Good News for Everyone!

Life-changing Encounters
in the Gospel of John

I0085451

By

Timothy J. Carlson

GUARDIAN
PUBLISHING, LLC

This edition published in May 2019 in association with

Guardian Publishing, LLC
Holt, Michigan

guardianpublishingllc.com

All Scripture quotations, unless otherwise noted, are taken from the Holy Bible: New International Version, 1984 (NIV), Copyright © 2002. Used by permission of the Zondervan Corporation, all rights reserved.

Acknowledgements

I begin by thanking those congregations who heard these studies, in sermon form, from their nascency through some fine-tuning. In particular, I dedicate this book to the membership of the Walnut Christian Church in Johnson City, Tennessee, and the membership of The Christian Church of East Sparta in East Sparta, Ohio.

Additionally, I express my thanks to my brother, Steven, for his publishing expertise which has been invaluable to me, as well as for his cover design. I also express gratitude to my nephew, Adam, whose editing skills were both helpful and necessary, and to Jo Anne McKinney for her grammatical assistance. Finally, I thank my wife, Patricia, for her support and encouragement through this tedious process.

Table of Contents

Preface

The material within these pages originated as messages prepared and presented to congregations where I have served as minister—namely the Walnut Christian Church (Johnson City, TN) where I served from 2005-2017 and The Christian Church of East Sparta (OH) where I presently minister. It is my hope that any fellow pulpiteers who peruse this volume will find some very "preachable" information within its pages.

Additionally, I hope that all who read this book will find these studies to possess a personal devotional purpose. I am confident that—as has been the case with me in studying and writing of them—each reader will find one or more of the personalities whose stories are the focus of these studies quite relatable to his or her own life narrative.

This book is also designed for facilitating group studies of its material; thus, the "Life Questions" at the conclusion of each chapter are intended to be launching pads for collective discussions among fellow-believers. Finally, my prayer is that all who journey through these pages will depart with a deeper knowledge of who the Savior is and will develop a greater appreciation of the difference he can continue to make in their lives.

Introduction to this Study

The apostle John wrote his gospel as an intimate portrait of Jesus. While there is some larger discourse material found in the fourth gospel (e.g. the Bread of Life Sermon and the temple discourse in chapters 6 and 7 as well as the elongated Upper Room teachings in chapters 13-16), the focus of John's portrait of Christ is personal. It is personal where John himself, "the disciple whom Jesus loved," is concerned, but it is also personal in regard to the interactions Jesus had with many other individuals whose stories are revealed in its pages.

John intentionally built his gospel around eight miracles performed by Jesus (other than his own resurrection) and these provide the thesis of his volume as stated in John 20:30: "...these are written that you may believe that Jesus is the Christ, the Son of God, and that by believing you may have life in his name." Yet John's is more than a gospel of "miracles;" it is also—certainly more so than the synoptics—a gospel of *conversations*. Some of the one-on-one dialogues that appear in this gospel are in the settings of miracles and with individuals for whom Jesus performed them, but many who experienced the privilege of a private audience with the Lord in John's record did not receive the additional benefit of a miracle. Nathaniel and Nicodemus did not. Neither did the woman at the well or the woman caught in adultery; yet perhaps what each of these received from the Lord was, for them, just as great as a physical miracle. Indeed, when one considers the very "miracle" that salvation is, with its eternal results, the offer that Jesus revealed to each of these was greater than any temporal, physical miracle.

Each of the personal encounters that John described are life-changing ones. None of these individuals Jesus met would or could ever be the same again. One would experience the Son of God's commendation for his evident genuineness. A Jewish religious leader would come face to face with his spiritual inadequacy. A despised and weary woman would experience acceptance and learn of "living water." An official would witness his son healed of a deadly fever simply by Jesus' spoken, long-distance word. A man incapable of walking for 38 years would be able to go wherever he wanted. A woman facing the death penalty for adultery would experience a dramatic, last-minute reprieve and—even more importantly—God's eternal forgiveness for her crime. A man who knew only darkness for his entire life would experience sight—both physical and spiritual—for the first time. Sorrowing sisters would receive their beloved brother back from death. A disciple who hesitated to believe the resurrection would become a herald of its reality. An apostle of the innermost circle would be restored from his fallenness and recommissioned in his most important calling.

As diverse as these individuals were in their backgrounds, stories, personalities and problems, the good news of the gospel touched each of them. Their diversity serves to remind us that the forgiving, healing, restoring, conquering, and hope-offering message of Christ is indeed "Good News for Everyone!"

Good News for the Sincere

—Nathaniel—

(John 1:43-51)

Introduction

The linguistic background of the word "sincere" is a noteworthy one. It comes from the combination of two Latin words: *sin*, meaning "without" and *cera*, meaning "wax." Its literal meaning then is "without wax." The word developed from the world of art— particularly from the art of sculpting—as wax was often used by sculptors in their creations to conceal defects to patch a chipped nose, a poorly shaped finger, etc. So, a sculpture that was "without wax" was a flawless piece of work. A sincere person, then, is one who has no hidden defects.[1]

We come across such an individual in John 1 in the person of Nathaniel (the disciple called "Bartholomew" in the synoptic gospels). I say he is "sincere" because that's what Jesus himself said about this man. The first observation Jesus made of him when he saw Nathaniel was to compliment him as "a true Israelite in whom there is nothing false." (John 1:47). The Greek word for "false", *dolos*, indicates someone who would trap another by deception. We know that Jesus' assessment of Nathaniel as a person without a deceptive bone in his body was true even though Jesus apparently had never met him before. This is because Jesus was God in the flesh and he knew everything about everyone—a truth that becomes evident throughout the gospel of John, as we shall see. In fact, John 2:25 states that

---

[1] Adapted from Paul Lee Tan, *Encyclopedia of 7,700 Illustrations* (Rockville, MD: Assurance Publishers, 1979), p. 1103.

4

Jesus "did not need man's testimony about man, for he knew what was in a man."

While Jesus possessed such supernatural knowledge that we cannot claim, I believe the testimony to Nathaniel's character becomes evident to us as well in the brief record that John provides us about him in this passage. In truth, what John recorded in this interaction between Jesus and Nathaniel comprises the virtual totality of what we know about Nathaniel from the gospels; yet these few verses reveal a lot about his genuine character to us.

Nathaniel chose a sincere friend.

While it is not a biblical statement, there is truth in the old axiom that claims "birds of a feather flock together." Nathaniel's friend was Philip, and from what we know of Philip (even though Jesus never specifically said this about him) he, too, was a person of sincerity. While the other early disciples seemed to "find" Jesus based upon John the Baptist's testimony of him, John 1:43 tells us that Jesus found Philip. That was no accident. The implication is that Philip—as Jesus could uniquely know—already possessed the kind of character Jesus was looking for in his followers. It was then Philip who told his friend Nathaniel about Jesus, identifying him as "the one Moses wrote about in the law, and about whom the prophets also wrote" (v. 45). Further, Philip is consistently presented in the gospels as one who wasn't afraid to express sincere thoughts (John 6:5-7 and 14:8) as well as sincerely involve himself in situations (John 12:20-22).

In our text, he proved to be a genuine friend to Nathaniel with whom he shared his newfound faith in Jesus. Proverbs 27:9 states "the pleasantness of one's friend springs from his earnest counsel." Those words describe the kind of friend Philip was toward Nathaniel. His counsel was to point his friend to Jesus; there is no better counsel any friend can give than this.

The quality of any of our characters can be seen in the kinds of friends we choose. Birds of a feather *do* flock together. The truthful character of Nathaniel is evident in the kind of friend he hung out with—specifically Philip, who was also clearly a sincere ("without wax") person.

Given that observation I feel compelled to ask: What could be said of *my* spiritual character based upon the friends I choose?

Nathaniel expressed sincere feelings.

When Philip told Nathaniel about the one whom they had found who fulfilled the descriptions of Moses and the prophets, he identified him as "Jesus of Nazareth, the son of Joseph." To this Nathaniel reacted with the visceral response: "Nazareth! Can anything good come from there?" (v. 46)

Why would Nathaniel make such a cynical statement and inquiry? Some suggest it was because he, as a student of Scripture, knew that the promised Messiah was to come from Bethlehem based on Micah 5:2, so he was reasoning, "How could the Messiah come from anywhere else?" (Of course, students of the gospel nativity narratives know the answer to that conundrum.) Others suggest—and I tend to agree with them—that Nathaniel, who, according to John 21:2, was from Cana in Galilee (note: this is the only other specific fact that we have about Nathaniel from the gospels), spoke this way because of his personal familiarity with the little village of Nazareth. Cana and Nazareth were very close to each other. One commentator writes:

> Nazareth held a poor reputation as a city. There was a certain contempt about Nazareth in other cities of Galilee because it was an insignificant and ruddy town. Maybe Nathaniel thought Jesus should have come from a major city like Jerusalem, not a rag-tag town like Nazareth. Nazareth was also theologically inconsequential in Scripture.[2]

---

[2] *Bible Exposition Commentary* at versebyversecommentary.com

Nathaniel expressed some understandable skepticism about Jesus here. The point regarding Nathaniel's questioning of Nazareth as a proper place from which the Messiah would hail is that he was expressing his genuine thoughts. His question revealed what was truly on his mind. He didn't hesitate to candidly state how he felt in response to Philip's claim.

Now we know that it is not always good just to say what one thinks or blurt out what is on one's mind. I like the old verse that reminds us:

> Just think before you take the floor
> The whale without a doubt,
> Would never feel the harpoon's steel
> If he didn't come up to spout!

Perhaps many of us could take the advice of Will Rogers who said one should "never miss a good chance to shut up." Yet, on the other hand, it's often refreshing to encounter people who genuinely speak their mind. These are those who just have nothing to hide. The refreshing thing about them is that you always know where they're coming from.

I remember one time when I, at the request of the elders in the church where I was ministering, preached a series of messages on church leadership. In it I focused on the biblical passages that revealed the roles and required character of those who would hold offices in the church. I am the first to admit that the series was quite academic and tedious.

After one of the duller sermons in the series, one of the ladies in the congregation who was known for not holding back in communicating her true feelings shook my hand and commented with one word: "Boooooring!" Okay, at first it hurt my feelings, but in short order I came to appreciate her honesty. It caused me to listen to her more because I knew when she complimented me, she also meant it. She expressed sincere feelings.

Too often we don't express our sincere feelings about things, and while it is good to be quiet sometimes, saying what we really think about things can, on occasion, be the right thing to do. Nathaniel demonstrated his genuineness by expressing his sincere feelings about Nazareth. It only underscores that with him there was no deception; in Nathaniel one got what one saw.

Nathaniel asked a sincere question.

When Jesus saw Nathaniel and declared of him as he approached, "Here is a true Israelite, in whom there is nothing false," Nathaniel was taken aback, and immediately asked of Jesus, "How do you know me?" (v. 48). Nathaniel recognized that Jesus had judged his character correctly. He didn't retort: "Rabbi—you've got me all wrong! I'm really a scoundrel!" His question as to Jesus' source of knowledge was a genuine one; he truly wanted a solution to the mystery of how Jesus knew him. Essentially, in discovering that Jesus seemed to know plenty about him, he now wanted to know more about Jesus, and so he asked this question.

I have discovered that not all questions people ask are sincere. This is true of even religious inquiries at times. I recently read about an incident that purportedly happened at a county fair where a distinctively dressed Quaker offered a horse for sale. A non-Quaker farmer asked its price and, since Quakers had a reputation for fair dealing, he bought the horse without hesitation. The farmer got the horse home, only to discover it was lazy and ill-tempered, so he took it back to the fair the next day. There he confronted the Quaker. "Thou hast no complaint against me," said the Quaker. "Had thou asked me about the horse, I would have told thee truthfully the problems, but thou didst not ask."

"That's okay," replied the farmer. "I don't want you to take the horse back. I want to try to sell him to someone else. Can I borrow your coat and hat for a while?"[3]

---

[3] Illustration from sermonsearch.org.

Just because something is cloaked in religious garb doesn't mean it is genuine. Sometimes people ask questions because they simply like to argue religion. Others, in my experience, have a tendency to raise questions about tangential issues of faith or obscure statements in the bible that have nothing to do with salvation. Often, it seems, these are inquiries to which the askers don't want the answers—or at least the *true* answers. I've discovered that frequently their motivation is not that of an earnest seeker, but one of avoidance of the weightier issues from God's revelation upon their lives.

Nathaniel, who was inherently sincere of heart, had his spiritual curiosity piqued by Jesus, and he immediately pursued a greater knowledge of this man from Nazareth. So, he asked a genuine question: "How do you know me?"

Nathaniel demonstrated sincere behavior.

Nathaniel's action reflecting sincere behavior was actually the *first* thing that he had done in this setting to demonstrate that there was nothing false in him. In truth, we don't even know specifically what behavior he had exhibited but, in answer to his question as to how Jesus knew him, the Savior brought it up with his enigmatic response: "I saw you while you were still under the fig tree before Philip called you." (v. 48)

While we don't know what Nathaniel was doing under that fig tree that caused Jesus to commend him for his genuineness, we might reflect on some possibilities: Was he deep in meditation over God's word with a scroll in his hands? Was that fig tree his closet of prayer away from the crowd where he had gone to talk alone with the Lord? Was he under the fig tree listening compassionately to a friend in need? Was he giving a significant gift of alms to a disabled beggar who regularly sat under the fig tree? Whatever he did there, his actions portrayed his sincerity of faith; Jesus witnessed it and commended him based upon it, and Nathaniel didn't disown the compliment. In fact, Jesus' truthful observation of him led him to believe in Jesus, which brings us to the final sincere act Nathaniel exhibited.

Nathaniel professed a sincere belief.

Verse 49 reveals Nathaniel's response to Jesus: "Then Nathaniel declared, 'Rabbi, you are the Son of God; you are the king of Israel.'" First, he addressed Jesus in immediate recognition of his authority as a spiritual teacher, calling him "rabbi." Then he acknowledged him as the very Son of God—Emmanuel who had come into their midst. Finally, he identified Jesus as the King of Israel---the long-awaited Messiah who would eternally sit on David's throne. This "true Israelite in whom there was nothing false" claimed Jesus as his personal king.

When you think about it, it is amazing to witness what a long distance Nathaniel came in a very short time. Just moments before he was sincerely questioning, "Nazareth! Can anything good come from there?" Now he's declaring Jesus of Nazareth to be God in the flesh, Israel's Messiah, and his Lord. Additionally, when you think about it, Nathaniel's profession of faith in Jesus is essentially the same profession of faith that we are required to make about him in the salvation response: that we believe he is the Messiah/Christ, God's Son and our Lord. It is noteworthy that, while Peter was commended by Jesus for first making this "good confession" in Matthew 16, Nathaniel made it long before Peter did. And while Jesus blessed Peter for receiving his confession, not through human reasoning "but by my Father in heaven" (Matthew 16:17), Nathaniel seems to have figured it out on his own, by the faithful reasoning of a sincere heart.

In his genuineness, Nathaniel readily surrendered to belief when confronted with undeniable truth about Jesus. Even Jesus seemed impressed by this, noting, "You believe because I told you I saw you under the fig tree..." Then he went on to reward his ready faith promising, "You shall see greater things than that...I tell you the truth, you shall see heaven open, and the angels of God ascending and descending on the Son of Man." (vv. 50-51). Nathaniel will be an eyewitness with the other apostles on occasions when heaven itself will place its approval upon Jesus (Matthew 3:17; John 12:28). He will hear the witness of heaven coming down in the very ministry of Jesus in the truths he will teach. He will, with the other apostles, witness Jesus' return to heaven in the presence of the heavenly angels (Acts 1:9-11).

Conclusion

Even as we focus on Nathaniel as one who was sincere in his friendship, feelings, curiosity, behavior, and beliefs, I am aware that, at least in some cases, sincerity may not be an all-encompassing virtue. We've all heard someone say, "One can be sincere, but one can also be *sincerely wrong*." While that may be true, if we take the word in its literal meaning "without wax," indicating not having a hint of deception, that also implies harboring no self-deception by a willingness to believe a lie. Nathaniel did not, nor would he, believe a lie. His truthful ideals would not allow him to do so. Thus, he immediately recognized Jesus for who he was and professed the same.

Jesus also recognized Nathaniel for who he was, and in a single phrase assessed him as "a true Israelite in whom there is nothing false," and he rewarded his sincere faith.

One may be left to wonder: What one-line assessment might Jesus make of me and you?

Life Questions

1. What friend in your life has had the most positive spiritual influence on you? _____

   _____

   _____

2. Who do you know now, or have you known in the past that, like Nathaniel, is sincere about expressing their thoughts and/or asking sincere questions? _____

_____

_____

Do you see this as a positive or negative characteristic in people?

_____

_____

_____

3. What criteria do you use in determining whether to speak your mind about something or keep your thoughts to yourself?

_____

_____

_____

_____

4. What are some possible things that Nathaniel might have been doing under the tree where Jesus saw him "before Philip called" him that led Jesus to commend him for his genuineness? _____

_____

_____

_____

5. What truths about Jesus did Nathaniel specifically profess? ____

_____

_____

How similar or dissimilar are these to the truths we are asked to profess about Jesus? _____

_____

_____

Good News for the Seeker

—Nicodemus—

(John 3:1-21)

Introduction

I once heard about a city that was celebrating its history. The richest man in town was asked to make a speech. As he spoke he bragged, "Fellow citizens, I want you to know how good this town has been to me. I was not originally from here, but I'll have you know that when I first came here 50 years ago, all I had was a dollar in my pocket and a knapsack over my shoulder, and today I am the richest man in town. This town has, indeed, been good to me!"

When he finished speaking, the crowd was in awe, then the emcee of the celebration turned to the man and said, "Well, sir, you have made us curious. If all you had was a dollar in your pocket, can you tell us what was in the knapsack you were carrying that day?"

The wealthy man replied pensively, "As I recall it contained five-thousand dollars in cash and one-hundred thousand dollars in government bonds."

Some people just seem to start out with advantages. In John 3 we meet such a person with whom Jesus had a very important conversation. His name was Nicodemus, and when he came to Jesus he did so from the perspective of spiritual advantage. Because his background was that of a religious leader and teacher in Israel, he was among those spiritually privileged persons of whom Jesus spoke in Matthew 13:52, when he declared, "Therefore every teacher of the law who has been instructed about the kingdom of heaven is like the owner of a house who brings out of his storeroom new treasures as well as old." Nicodemus came to Jesus with the old treasure of having intimate knowledge of the Scriptures and God's law as well

13

as a personal dedication to them. He brought with him an understanding and expectation of God's promised kingdom; but he was about to add to his storeroom some new treasures/truths that he would learn from Jesus.

The Trust Nicodemus Demonstrated

John begins this narrative by telling us in 3:1-2,

> Now there was a man of the Pharisees named Nicodemus, a member of the Jewish ruling council. He came to Jesus at night and said, "Rabbi, we know you are a teacher who has come from God. For no one could perform the miraculous signs you are doing if God were not with him."

Why Nicodemus came to Jesus at night can only be a matter of conjecture since the text doesn't tell us. It seems to me there are two possible reasons as to why he did this: first, out of fear; or second, out of a desire for more attention.

In the first case he may have met Jesus in the dark for fear of his fellow Jewish religious leaders from whom he sought to hide his assessment of Jesus. (We should note here that in the profession of faith with which he commenced his conversation with Jesus, Nicodemus indicated that he was not alone in his assessment. Using the first-person plural, he asserted, "we know you are a teacher sent from God." Yet, while we do later meet another such person with whom Nicodemus is associated in the gospel of John—Joseph of Arimathea in John 19:38-39—we can be certain that those among the Jewish leaders who professed any kind of faith in Jesus were few and far between, and those who did so would not have met with the approval of the leadership as a whole.)

In the second case Nicodemus may have sought an audience at night so he could, out of a genuine desire to learn, have Jesus to himself away from the daytime crowds that surrounded the Lord. Or, of course, both of these reasons may have been at play in Nicodemus' choice of setting for speaking with Jesus.

We must not miss the fact that Nicodemus began with a profession of faith. Like Nathaniel, he addressed Jesus as "rabbi," indicating a personal honor of him as a teacher of the Scriptures. Although Nicodemus didn't go as far as Nathaniel in noting his identity as God's Son and the Messiah, he acknowledged his belief—along with that of others who agreed with him—that Jesus was sent from God, this being based upon the miracles he had performed.

It is possible that Nicodemus had heard about the one specific miracle of Jesus recorded to this point: his changing the water into wine at the village of Cana. It is probable that he was among the "many people [who] saw the miraculous signs he was doing" while he was at Jerusalem during the Feast of Passover (John 2:23). Whatever were the signs to which this seeker was referring, Nicodemus unhesitatingly expressed his trust that Jesus was "from God" because of these demonstrations of his power.

What exactly Jesus' being "from God" meant to this religious seeker at this point is unclear. We can be sure that Nicodemus' intent in coming to Jesus was to find out more about the identity of this rabbi from Nazareth based upon this assessment. It is important to note that, upon granting Jesus this compliment, whatever questions Nicodemus intended to ask him were never uttered. Yet, my guess is, whatever they were they were all answered, and he likely learned even more and greater truths about Jesus from Jesus than he had imagined he would.

The Truths that Jesus Taught
Jesus cut Nicodemus off at his compliment. He didn't disagree with him, for if anyone knew that he was indeed "a teacher who has come from God," Jesus himself knew that. Nor did Jesus take time to agree with or thank him for his compliment; rather, he simply built on it by proceeding to teach Nicodemus some important truths he had brought from God.

In the conversation that follows, which includes the most quoted verse in all of the bible, Jesus revealed two grand truths about the kingdom of God: one has to do with the *entering* of it by the individual and the other has to do with the *extending* of it by God to men through his love and mercy.

Regarding the entering of the kingdom of God, Jesus taught Nicodemus that the individual desiring to do so must experience two things: first, he or she must be "born again...of the water and the Spirit;" second, he or she must believe in the One whom God has sent who will make possible the salvation proffered through the kingdom. In my understanding, being "born of water" certainly intimates Christian baptism—an action of submission that is consistently scripturally required for salvation (Mark 16:16; Acts 2:38; Romans 6:3-4; I Peter 3:21)---while being "born of the Spirit" involves surrendering to the activities of the Spirit involved in conversion; these include following the Holy Spirit's conviction of us in the salvation process (John 15:26; 16:5-7), receiving his indwelling presence at baptism (Acts 2:38), then submitting to his guidance in our lives (Galatian 5:16).

As noted, the second requirement for one entering the kingdom is expressed belief in the identity and work of Jesus as God's Son. He is the One who was sent into the world out of his Father's love to redeem us so that no one should perish. Jesus revealed to Nicodemus that the act of believing in him was prefigured in the lifting up of the bronze serpent by Moses in the wilderness as recorded in Numbers 21:4-9. This was when the Israelites complained about their plight in the desert regarding the lack of food and water there and of the manna God was sending them daily for which they were developing a growing distaste. In response, God sent serpents among them and many Israelites died from their venomous bites. To save the people, God instructed Moses to "Make a [bronze] snake and put it on a pole; anyone who is bitten can look at it and live." Jesus' point was that when we, in the same way, look to him by faith as God's means of salvation from sin, we too will survive the venom of sin's condemnation, which is death. So, the one who believes in Jesus "shall not perish, but have eternal life."

The second great aspect of truth in Jesus' words to Nicodemus regards God's role in all of this as he extends his kingdom to us. While we are required to surrender by baptism and belief, God is doing his part as well. In fact, God's part in all of this is the far greater part: he sent his Son into the world to be lifted up; he orchestrated for his Son to be sacrificed for our sins; he provided (and provides) the person and presence of the Holy Spirit in the world and in our lives to facilitate our submission to him. In short, Jesus revealed to Nicodemus—and to us by way of Scripture—that the opportunity to enter the kingdom that God has gone out of his way to extend to us is ours for the choosing.

Whatever Nicodemus planned to ask Jesus that night is never revealed to us, but no issue could have been more important than the subject matter Jesus taught him about: his need to respond to the kingdom that God was extending to him. In reality, no issue in life could be more important than this issue for anyone.

The Truths We Can Take Away

You can't be too respected to need Jesus. Nicodemus was a man of position. He was a leading Pharisee who was honored to be a member of the ruling Jewish Council, the Sanhedrin. Paul T. Butler, in his commentary on the gospel of John, reminds us that this council "had religious jurisdiction over every Jew in the world."[4] Wherever Nicodemus went he was admired. His very name used here (which was Greek and certainly not his original Jewish name) meant one who was "a conqueror of people." Perhaps that indicates he had the personality of one who knew "how to win friends and influence people" long before the self-help book of that title was ever imagined.

---

[4] Paul T. Butler, *The Gospel of John, Vol. 1* (Joplin, MO: College Press, 1985), p. 93.

Yet, when he came to Jesus as a man of such position and power, Jesus confronted him with his insufficiency. While he had done well at people-pleasing, he was not fully pleasing to God. All of what he had in regard to position and authority meant nothing when it came to entering the kingdom of God. Just like everyone else, he would have to be born (again) of the water and the Spirit; he would have to submit to faith in Jesus as God's Son.

You can't be too knowledgeable to need Jesus. Nicodemus was a scholar who knew the Scriptures intimately; he also knew by rote the traditions by which the Jews interpreted them. He was a rabbi in his own right as a teacher of Israel. In fact, Jesus didn't merely call him "*a* teacher of Israel," but, according to the original Greek, he addressed Nicodemus as "*the* teacher of Israel." The implication is that this man was dominant among the Jewish teachers and scholars of his day. He was very knowledgeable about religious matters and was used to answering the questions of others; but this man came to Jesus to have his questions answered. Although perhaps not to his expectations, they were answered for him by the Savior, and in part the point of what Jesus had to say was to reveal to Nicodemus that all of his learning could not save him; he needed to be born again and believe in God's Son.

You can't be too mature to need Jesus. Nicodemus was not a young man when he came to Jesus at night. Members of the Sanhedrin were graybeards. They were men who had reached years of maturity through which they had gained the respect and trust of the people. Likewise, Nicodemus' status as a leading teacher in Israel would only have been achieved through many years of learning and teaching. Yet, even with all his years and the religious experience that accompanied them, Nicodemus needed more—he needed a Savior.

In our culture we tend to think of conversion to Christ as happening only or primarily in the season of youth. A 2015 study by the National Association of Evangelicals showed that 63% of all American conversions take place before the age of 15. Another 34%

are converted by the age of 29, which means only 3% of conversions to Christ take place at the age of 30 or above.[5] This is observably true when you think about it; rarely do we witness persons coming to Christ beyond that age—in their 40s, 50s or later. (The oldest person I ever baptized was 77.) But the need for Jesus is present in the life of everyone at any age.

I once came across an adaptation of the children's song *Jesus Loves Me*. It was written by a man named Bob Wilson and is entitled *Jesus Loves Older Folk, Too*. It includes these verses:

Jesus loves me this I know,
Though my hair is white as snow,
Though my sight is growing dim,
Still he bids me trust in Him.

Though my steps are oh so slow,
With my hand in His I'll go,
On through life let come what may,
He'll be there to lead the way

When my work on earth is done
And life's victories are won,
He will take me home above
To learn the fullness of His love.

Yes, Jesus loves me,
Yes, Jesus loves me,
Yes, Jesus loves me,
The Bible tells me so.[6]

Indeed, we possess the need for Jesus at any age. Whatever are the number of years represented by the candles on your birthday cake, it is never too late to turn to him and experience his saving benefits.

---

[5] Reported at www.nae.net/when-americans-become-christians.
[6] Bob Wilson at www.bobwilsonmusic.org.

You can't be too good to need Jesus. For all of the negative impressions we have of them from the gospels, it is important to know that the Pharisees were serious about their religion. They really sought to do what they thought was God's will where the law was concerned. They would do things like fast twice a week and give the money they saved from not eating to the poor. Jesus held them up as the challenging model of righteousness that we need to surpass in order to enter the kingdom. In what many consider to be the thesis statement to the Sermon on the Mount in Matthew 5:20, Jesus declared: "For I tell you that unless your righteousness surpasses that of the Pharisees and teachers of the law, you will certainly not enter the kingdom of heaven." To be sure, there was a lot of legalism and hypocrisy practiced among them, and Jesus strongly condemned them for these things; yet the Pharisees took the pursuit of righteousness seriously. Still, all of the practical goodness that they attained by their exercised and imposed interpretations of God's law did not result in placing them in good standing with God. This is because no person's practical goodness on any level can save him or her. Only God's grace extended through his Son can accomplish this. It is safe to assume that Nicodemus was a good and very moral man. I believe he was probably even an exception among the Pharisees as to hypocritical ways, but he still needed Jesus. He needed his sacrifice. He needed to say yes to the love of God expressed through the gift of his Son.

Conclusion

Unlike Nathaniel, of whom the biblical details are virtually entirely revealed in his conversation with Jesus in John 1, we do have a bit more information about Nicodemus in the Scriptures. In John 7, when the temple guards who had been sent to arrest Jesus returned with a positive assessment of him claiming, "No one ever spoke the way this man does," the leaders stood ready to condemn Jesus and his followers, noting of those who were believing in Jesus, "there is a curse on them." (v. 49). Here Nicodemus defended Jesus and his followers by insisting to the Council, "Does our law condemn anyone without first hearing him to find out what he is doing?" At his question they temporarily backed off.

Nicodemus also appeared after the death of Jesus in John 19:38-40. Here the gospel writer tells us that he assisted Joseph of Arimathea in burying the body of Jesus. Nicodemus himself paid for the expensive mixture of myrrh and aloes with which they anointed the Lord's body.

Sadly, this is the last word we have about Nicodemus in the Scriptures. I'd like to point to a text in the book of Acts where he is mentioned as an active participant in the early church, but we do not find any such passage. I'd like to be able to point out some early church traditions that have been handed down to us about Nicodemus which reveal his continued following of Christ after the resurrection, but there are no credible ones. This is not to say that he wasn't there—that he didn't go from being a secretive believer to publicly professing his faith in Jesus as a teacher sent from God, God's incarnate Son and his Savior. In fact, it's hard for me to imagine him being so close to all of the events of the crucifixion and resurrection, as well as his demonstrated interest in Jesus, and his not becoming a full convert to the faith. But it is possible, I suppose, that he didn't become a Christian in the end, and it is perhaps significant that we possess no record of him beyond John 19.

I find this sad because I know that if he didn't finish in the Lord, the hope that Jesus spoke of to him could never be his to claim. All the things Nicodemus did—from initially expressing his faith in Jesus to his assistance in burying the Lord's body—would have been for naught if he did not continue in his belief. The good news that Jesus offered this seeker who came to him by night required a lifetime of response. It requires the same for us.

Are you giving God a lifetime of response for what he has done for you? After all, he so loved *you* (and *me*) "that he gave his one and only Son, that whoever believes in him shall not perish but have eternal life."

Life Questions

1. What is the meaning of the name "Nicodemus?" _____
   _____
   _____

   How might this name fit his character? _____
   _____
   _____

2. How does Jesus seem to portray Nicodemus as a very prominent teacher among the Jews in his time? _____
   _____
   _____

3. Who is the oldest person you have known to come to faith in Christ? _____ At what age did this person experience their conversion? _____ At what age did you come to Christ? _____

4. What would you say to a person who refuses to see his/her need for salvation in Christ based on confidence in his/her own moral goodness? _____
   _____
   _____
   _____

Good News for the Social Outcast

—The Woman at the Well—

(John 4:4-26)

Introduction

Of all the one-on-one encounters that Jesus had in the gospel of John as he shared the good news with a variety of people—indeed of all the personal encounters that Jesus experienced in all of the gospels—this one is, without a doubt, the most surprising. We can understand why Jesus would commence a conversation with Nathaniel, "an Israelite in whom there was nothing false;" and we can appreciate the fact that Jesus would take time with Nicodemus, the seeker who came to Jesus by night and was a religious leader ("*the* teacher" among the Jews). Jesus had some common starting points with these men, but the woman at the well is a different story. She represented the polar opposite of what we would expect of a candidate for becoming a disciple of Jesus. Jesus did encounter other notably sinful people who either came to him willingly (e.g. the woman who anointed Jesus in Luke 7 and Zacchaeus, the tax collector, in Luke 19) or unwillingly (e.g. the woman caught in the act of adultery in John 8), but it is apparent that Jesus personally sought out the woman at the well. He met up with her intentionally in this setting. *He* began the conversation with *her*.

Who this Woman Was

I suggest that this was the most surprising personal encounter that Jesus had with anyone in the gospels because of who this woman was. There is a true sense in which, because of who she was, the conversation revealed to us in John 4 never should have

23

occurred. It happened because Jesus chose for it to happen despite the social obstacles that would have forbidden it. The woman at the well, as we shall see, was a social outcast on many levels.

First, *she was a **gender** outcast*. Women in general were treated with low regard in ancient Near Eastern cultures, and there was certainly no exception to this reality among the Jews of Jesus' day. In fact, in some ways they may have gone further than many other cultures in their negative esteem of women—especially when in the public arena. Paul Butler elaborates on this:

> No Jew would speak to any woman in public—not even his own wife or daughter. This foolish tradition was carried to such an extreme that some Pharisees would close their eyes when they saw a woman on the streets. As a result, they often bumped into walls and houses, and they became known as "the bruised and bleeding Pharisees."[1]

To me that sounds like a high price to pay in order not to make eye contact with someone. It is obvious from this passage, as well as from many other public encounters in the gospels Jesus had with women, that our Lord didn't buy into this charade. He didn't practice it and he didn't teach it—or anything like it—to be practiced among his followers. Yet, especially with this woman of Sychar, Jesus seems to break down the gender wall that would have divided them.

Second, *she was a **racial** outcast*. This woman was a Samaritan. The Samaritans were a mixed race of people who lived in a relatively small geographical area around what had been the capitol of the northern kingdom of Israel in the Old Testament: Samaria. That kingdom, as you may recall, was destroyed by the nation of Assyria in 722 BC. Per the conquering custom of the Assyrians, they dispersed most of the people of Israel to other subjugated regions of their empire leaving behind only the poorest remnant in the land, then they relocated other conquered populations into the Israelite

---

[1] Paul T. Butler, *The Gospel of John, Vol. 1*, pp. 142-143.

territory. Intermarrying and cultural and religious synthesis subsequently occurred between these forced neighbors, thus forming this blended race. (Please note that the interesting record of the Samaritans' beginnings is found in 2 Kings 17:24-41.)

Because they were a mixed race and not of genuine Israelite lineage, they were not accepted by those who legitimately could claim to be descendants of Jacob. So, the Jews of Jesus' day harbored a centuries-old prejudice toward the Samaritans. Interestingly—as prejudice usually does—it went both ways between the Jews and the Samaritans. When Jesus was passing through the Samaritan region, as he was heading toward Jerusalem in Luke 9, he sent messengers ahead to a Samaritan village through which he and his disciples were about to pass. Verse 53 reveals the reciprocal prejudice of these inhabitants toward the Jews: "but the people there did not welcome him, because he was heading for Jerusalem." (This was when the two "sons of thunder," James and John, wanted to call fire down from heaven to destroy the people of this village, which led, of course, to Jesus' rebuke of them.)

Jesus refused to participate in the practice of mutual prejudice that existed between these two races of people. He exemplified this refusal for his disciples, and I am confident that he continues to be intolerant of racial prejudice on any level among his followers today. Thus, Jesus would even elevate a Samaritan to a heroic role in the parable of the good Samaritan (Luke 10:30-37), and he would credit a uniquely thankful man who had received healing from leprosy— among nine others (presumably Jews) who did not express thanks— in Luke 17, the gospel writer noting that this man "was a Samaritan." (Luke 17:16). Considering the depth of this prejudice in Jesus' day, the evident surprise of the woman at Jacob's Well in verse 9 is understandable: "You are a Jew and I am a Samaritan woman. How can you ask me for a drink?"

The parenthetical editorial comment that John offers (and he frequently offers these throughout his gospel) at the end of verse 9 is insufficiently translated, "For Jews do not associate with

Samaritans." The NIV Study Bible footnote offers the alternative: "(Jews) do not use dishes Samaritans have used." The Greek indicates that Jews had "no use for" Samaritans. *The Message* interprets the meaning bluntly: "Jews in those days wouldn't be caught dead talking to Samaritans."[2] But Jesus would; and he did, thus breaking down the wall of racial prejudice with this woman.

Third, *she was a* **religious** *outcast.* Just as the Samaritans were mixed racially, their religion was also a mixture of the worship of Jehovah and idolatrous practices that had been introduced from the pagan side of their ancestry. To the Jews this was perceptively worse than the practice of outright idolatry. It was a form of blasphemy of the God of Israel as it diminished—even mocked—the true worship of him. As we learn later in Jesus' conversation with this woman, the Samaritans viewed themselves in their religion to be in competition, of sorts, with the Jewish religious system; they even had their own temple on Mount Gerizim just outside the city of Sychar where this woman lived.

The religious hostility between these two peoples also had centuries of history behind it. When the Jewish exiles returned from Babylon and began rebuilding the temple in Jerusalem in 536 BC, those who lived in the region of Samaria were not allowed to assist in this project under the leadership of Zerubbabel due to their religious impurity. These "enemies" then tried to sabotage the Jews' efforts in constructing the temple as well as in their later endeavors to rebuild Jerusalem (Ezra 4:1-24). In 444 BC, when the Jews under Nehemiah began rebuilding the walls of Jerusalem, Samaritan leaders were among those who tried to stop them in that task as well (Nehemiah 2:19; 4:1-15).

The woman encountered by Jesus in John 4 identified with the religious system of the Samaritans, noting that the fathers (of her and those living in that region) "worshiped on this mountain" (in the temple on Mt. Gerizim). Additionally, she referenced the continuing

---

[2] Eugene H. Peterson, *The Message//Remix: The Bible in Contemporary Language* (Colorado Springs, CO: Navpress, 2003), p. 1931.

religious rivalry her people sensed with the Jews who insisted, as she stated, "that the place where we must worship is in Jerusalem." (v. 20). Yet, even her identity as a religious outcast to the Jews didn't stop Jesus from building a bridge to her for her own good.

The animosity between Jews and Samaritans was so strong that most Jews, when traveling from Galilee to Judea or, as Jesus was, from Judea to Galilee, would avoid the region of Samaria altogether. To accomplish this, they would go many miles out of their way over to the Jordan Valley on the east to traverse northward or southward around Samaria. But Jesus didn't do this. In fact, in the gospels he appears consistently to go through the Samaritan territory on his journeys between these two Jewish regions. Curiously, John 4:4 states, "...he had to go through Samaria." Perhaps it is meant for us to understand that for Jesus it was, in the plan of the Father, necessary for him to break the tradition of bypassing Samaria, which was based in hostility and prejudice, so that he could sow some seeds of the gospel in that region—which is exactly what he did, beginning with this woman at Jacob's Well.

Fourth, *she was a **spiritual** outcast*. Certainly, she would have been such for the Jews based on all of the aforementioned reasons, but also based upon what we subsequently learn of her: that she had been married five times and now was living with a man without the benefit of marriage (vv. 17-18). When you think about it, if, as later revealed in John 8, the Jewish religious leaders were more than ready to stone a woman of their own identity for singularly being caught in the act of adultery, how much more would they have been storing up rocks for this Samaritan woman?

While she would have been a spiritual outcast to the Jews, it is more than probable that her moral choices also left her as a spiritual outcast among her own people. Perhaps this is why we find her at the well by herself in the midst of the day. Normally this would have been a place of considerable social interaction. The village women would have—as women are wont to do—traveled in groups the half-mile distance outside of town to the well; but who among them would

27

want to be seen with such a woman? Perhaps it is that Jesus chose to speak with this woman of Sychar because no one else there would.

What the Savior Did

Despite her identity as an outcast in these many ways, Jesus connected with her, and the model that he used to communicate his good news with her serves for us as a challenging example as to how we, when positioned to do so, may share his saving message with the outcasts of our own world.

Jesus met her in a casual setting. The Lord met this woman on her turf in a locale where she would normally be. This well was a place that she regularly came to meet a daily need.

When I was a boy the evangelistic program of my home church was accomplished through a monthly "Calling Night" in which the leaders and several volunteers of our congregation would go out and knock on doors in the community. This was often done in the fashion of cold calling (just showing up at someone's doorstep) to invite them to church and to have spiritual discussions. This approach was quite successful in the rural culture of the 1960s in which I was raised. For the most part evangelism in our culture doesn't work well that way today. While in the intervening years a lot of emphasis has been placed on seeker-friendly churches (in which unsaved people gravitate to us because we portray intentionally inviting and comfortable atmospheres in our worship services), presently, and with some reaction to the seeker model, the best evangelism seems to occur on the relational level. It is accomplished by shared personal faith from one individual to another, from a Christian to a non-Christian, when believers connect with unbelievers. This best occurs in casual settings with casual conversations, whether with a co-worker in the break room, a waitress at a restaurant, the neighbor across the backyard fence or the fellow teammate after practice.

I personally believe that the best evangelism always has occurred in this way. Jesus himself revealed this as a style of sharing the gospel. It is even evident in the Great Commission that he gave us

28

in Matthew 28:19-20. Despite the assumption implied by most of our translations that Jesus commanded us to "Go" and make disciples, the imperative does not lie in that word in the Greek. The actual command is to "make disciples" while the word "go" is a participle. It is perhaps best translated as a participle of time, the intent being "as you go...disciple people." (It is thus translated in the International Standard Version [ISV Foundation, 2011] of the bible.) Considering Jesus' model of evangelism in the gospels it is evident that he not only taught this method of sharing the gospel on-the-way, he also exemplified it as he met people who needed to hear his good news and taught them of it in the common settings of their lives. Thus, he spoke of the living water he could offer to a woman who had come in pursuit of water for physical replenishment.

Jesus took risks. As we have noted, even speaking to a woman in public was a risk for a Jewish man—especially for a rabbi and with a woman of this background and known character. Jesus even dared to be alone with her as his disciples had journeyed to another location to secure food supplies. He also dared to ask her for a favor by requesting her to give him a drink. While it is hard to imagine Jesus ever being outside of his comfort zone with any human being (he was, after all, God in the flesh and the very Creator of life), meeting with this woman likely came as close to this as any such circumstance for him. But for Jesus, any risk he was taking with her was much less important than the purpose of planting the seed of the gospel in her life.

Jesus elicited her curiosity. This part of the narrative unfolds in verses 10-15:

> Jesus answered her, "If you knew the gift of God and who it is that asks you for a drink, you would have asked him and he would have given you living water."

> "Sir," the woman said, "you have nothing to draw with and the well is deep. Where can you get this water? Are you greater than our father Jacob, who gave us the well and

drank from it himself, as did also his sons and his flocks and herds?"

Jesus answered, "Everyone who drinks this water will be thirsty again, but whoever drinks the water I give him will never thirst. Indeed, the water I give him will become in him a spring of water welling up to eternal life."

The woman said to him, "Sir, give me this water so that I won't get thirsty and have to keep coming here to draw water."

A familiar old story relates the account of a man who bought a mule from a rather shrewd farmer. (Yes, in some ways it is similar to the one I previously related about the Quaker who sold the horse.) The farmer assured the purchaser that the mule was well-trained and responsive. However, the first time that the man tried to work the mule, he was unsuccessful in getting it to do anything he instructed. With each command the mule remained as still as a statue. Finally, in total frustration, the man telephoned the farmer to help solve the problem.

When the farmer arrived on the scene, he gave the mule the same commands that the man had given---with the exact same outcome. The mule ignored all attempts at persuasion. Finally, the farmer picked up a two-by-four and dealt the creature a terrific blow across the forehead. He then gave a command which the mule followed immediately.

Having witnessed this, the mule's new owner was extremely upset. "You told me that this mule was well-trained and obedient," he declared, "and now you have to hit him over the head to get him going! How can you say that he is obedient?"

"Oh, he is obedient," the farmer insisted. "He does whatever you say. You just have to get his attention first."

By introducing the curious subject of "living water" that he can offer her, Jesus creatively got this woman's attention in this setting. When she heard of this substance, she had to learn more about it.

Not understanding that Jesus was using this as a metaphor for the salvation he offers, she responded in hope that this would be a source of provision that would render needless her daily, lonely and labor-intensive journey to the well. In reality Jesus was offering her something far greater than this, but he used this point of interest to open the door to teach her deeper truths.

I once heard about a class on missions at a bible college in which the meaning of the text "You are the salt of the earth," was being discussed. Several suggestions were given. "Salt imparts a desirable flavor," said one.

Another suggested, "Salt preserves from decay."

Finally, one young female student made an observation none of the others had thought of: "Salt creates thirst," she said.

There was a sudden hush over the class as students began to reflect, "Have I ever made anyone thirsty for the Lord?"

In this encounter Jesus caused the woman of Sychar—thirsty for physical water as she was—to become aware of her spiritual thirst. We often have the same challenge regarding those with whom we would share the gospel today and, like Jesus, we often need to begin by getting their attention in creative ways.

Jesus confronted her sin. The conversation continues in verses 16-18:

> He told her, "Go, call your husband and come back."
>
> "I have no husband," she replied.
>
> Jesus said to her, "You are right when you say you have no husband. The fact is, you have had five husbands, and the man you now have is not your husband. What you have said is quite true."

Confronting sinful behavior is not something a lot of Christians— or churches for that matter—are comfortable with these days. This is true whether one is speaking of the sins of individuals or addressing sin on the cultural level. In many cases it is considered too "politically

31

incorrect" to identify sin for what God has clearly revealed that it is. Perhaps, on the personal level, we tend to fear that when we address others' sins our own pet sins will become a fair target in the discussion. Of course, we know that Jesus—unlike us—had no such sins of which to be legitimately accused.

As is evident from this encounter, when sharing the good news of the gospel Jesus did not hesitate to confront the reality of sin in the lives of people. We must not, either. Indeed, it is fair to ask: how can the required ordinance of repentance of sin in response to the gospel ever be acted upon if the reality and shame of sinful behavior is not first confronted?

Jesus answered her questions. Perhaps understandably this woman changed the subject of the conversation in verses 19-20. So, sensing that Jesus was a true prophet (because of what he had revealed to her about her) she raised the hotly debated issue between the Samaritans and Jews regarding the proper place to worship. Was it here at the temple on Mt. Gerizim or at the Jewish temple in Jerusalem?

Jesus resolved the dilemma of this debate in three steps: first, he told her that her religion—the belief system of the Samaritans—was *wrong* by stating, "You Samaritans worship what you do not know." Jesus was averring that, despite their claimed traditions, her people had no divine revelation on which to stand for their religious practices or the presence of their temple. (How politically incorrect in our proudly pluralistic society would it be to say, as Jesus does here, that someone else's religion is *wrong?*)

Second, Jesus revealed that the religion of the Jewish people was reasonably based in divine revelation by stating, "We worship what we do know." (They knew it because God legitimately had spoken to them through the law and the prophets of the Old Testament.)

Finally, Jesus noted that the purpose of this genuine religion was to point to something greater: "for," he continued, "salvation is from the Jews." Then, in verses 23-24, he revealed what will be the end result of that something greater (i.e. the salvation resulting from his work and passion) in regard to the worship question she had raised:

> Yet a time is coming and has now come when true worshipers will worship the Father in spirit and truth, for they are the kind of worshipers the Father seeks. God is spirit and his worshipers must worship in spirit and in truth.

What was Jesus' answer to the Samaritan woman's question as to the correct locale of worship? At the present Jerusalem was the right place to worship, but there would shortly be a time, with the establishment of the new covenant, when the place of worship in regard to a physical edifice would not be what matters; the greater concern would be the substance of (the *truth* of worship) and the sincerity of and reasons for worshiping God (the *spirit* of worship). I can only imagine that with this answer the woman saw that Jesus had transcended the heated topic of debate and taught a significant new truth to her.

Finally, *Jesus revealed his identity to her.* Having had her worship concern addressed by Jesus, the woman brought up another pertinent religious topic of the day: the coming Messiah. Their recorded conversation concludes in verses 25-26:

> The woman said, "I know that Messiah (called Christ) is coming. When he comes he will explain everything to us."
>
> Then Jesus declared, "I who speak to you am he."

With this statement Jesus shared with her the heart of the gospel message—the truth of his identity as the Messiah. This was a unique declaration by Jesus to this Samaritan woman. There is no record of Jesus just coming out and saying this even to his close disciples; they had to figure it out on their own by witnessing his ministry and, in Peter's case, by experiencing a little divine assistance to do so (Matthew 16:17). Additionally, this woman became one of the first

33

persons to proclaim the gospel message based on Jesus' revelation about himself to her.

John's record continues in verses 28-29: "Then, leaving her water jar, the woman went back to the town and said to the people, 'Come see a man who told me everything I ever did. Could this be the Christ?'" Jesus' words had so affected her that she left the water jar she had come to the well to fill. She also exaggerated when she claimed to the townspeople that he had "told her everything she ever did." (In reality he didn't; it just may have *felt* like he did and, from what he did tell her, she knew he *could* have told it all.) Finally, her phrase, "Could this be the Christ?" is not a question in the traditional sense; it carries the implication of personal affirmation on her part. It may be rendered, "Surely this is the Christ!" It was a proclamation of the gospel message from a believer to unbelievers. This immoral Samaritan woman could legitimately lay claim to being one of the original preachers of the gospel!

Conclusion

The story of the woman at the well didn't end when she returned to town. In a sense, that's when her story truly began because, upon returning, she became a successful evangelist in her village. Verse 39 informs us that "Many of the Samaritans from that town believed in him because of the woman's testimony." When the people there persuaded Jesus to remain at their village for a couple of days, we subsequently learn that "many more became believers" because of Jesus' own words to them (v. 41).

But her story didn't end there, either. In Acts 1:8 Jesus informed his disciples that they will be witnessing for him "in all...Samaria" which, of course, would include Sychar. In Acts chapter 8 Philip the evangelist was first to go to this region proclaiming the now-fulfilled gospel. His success was so great that the church in Jerusalem sent the apostles Peter and John to help out with the work. While I can't state it with absolute certainty, I cannot help but believe that the success of the work in the region of the Samaritans all began with the groundwork that had been laid there a few years before when Jesus encountered a woman—one who in almost every way she could have been was an outcast—at Jacob's Well, and he asked her, "Will you give me a drink?"

If you think of yourself as a social outcast, know that the gospel is for you. If you know someone who is considered a social outcast, rest assured that the gospel is for them. Meet them where they are. Be willing to take risks with them. Creatively pique their interest regarding their spiritual needs. Confront their sinfulness as necessary. Answer their religious questions; and, most importantly, tell them who Jesus is.

Life Questions

1. What kinds of persons might be considered "outcasts" in our society today? _____
   _____
   _____

2. What are some social encounters that you experience that might be fertile opportunities for sharing your faith with someone? __
   _____
   _____
   _____
   _____

3. What is the most creative method you have ever heard of (or been involved in yourself) for sharing the gospel with someone? ____
   _____
   _____
   _____
   _____

4. Have you ever felt the need to confront someone about their sinful behavior? _____ If so, and you followed through, do you consider your effort to have been successful? _____

Why or why not?_____

_____

_____

Good News for the Submissive

—The Royal Official—

(John 4:43-54)

Introduction

When I was a senior in college, I had a car accident on a snowy road. Fortunately, there were no injuries and the car remained drivable. Unfortunately, the car was old and it was technically totaled. With the insurance payoff my dad decided to fix the car for me, putting on several new parts (a front bumper, grill, fender and hood) and having a body shop paint it. I would pick up the car when I came home for spring break, which I did. While I was there, I needed to do a little tweaking on the hood latch of the car, so I asked my dad to borrow his vice grip. (This is as any good son does—only I always returned his tools when I borrowed them.) He informed me that he didn't know where it was and that he hadn't been able to find it when he had recently needed it. Shortly he bought a new vice grip tool.

A couple years later, after I had graduated college and was settled into a full-time ministry with a small church, I was still driving that car and one day, while working underneath it, I looked up and saw the end of it; it was still attached to a bolt on the inside of the bumper: my dad's long-lost vice grip! Apparently, he had left it clamped there when he bolted the bumper onto the car. My first thought was that he must have clamped it there very tightly because it had been traveling like that for about 30,000 miles by that time. Then I notice how rusted it was and wondered if I could salvage it. Well, I did salvage it. I cleaned it up, greased it and had it looking and working like new. The next time I went to visit my dad I gladly—and much to his surprise after the ensuing years—returned his long-lost vice grip to him.

37

Have you ever found something in a place that you didn't expect to find it? In John 4 I think we do. Specifically, it is a virtue that we find. At that, it is a virtue that is compatible with the kingdom of God. But we find it in a place—or more specifically, a person—where and in whom we may be surprised to find it. It is the virtue of humility and we find it in one no less than a royal official. I say it is a kingdom virtue because Jesus taught that it was. In the first beatitude he declared, "Blessed are the poor in spirit, for theirs is the kingdom of heaven" (Matthew 5:3). Additionally, he taught the beatitude, "Blessed are the meek, for they will inherit the earth." (Matthew 5:5). Jesus also instructed his disciples of the necessity of becoming like a child in order to enter the kingdom (Mark 10:13-15), and he insisted, in response to their rivalry about position in the kingdom, that the greatest among them would be the servant of all (Matthew 20:20-26).

Humility is a primary kingdom virtue and the royal official of John 4 clearly possessed and demonstrated it. We don't know who this official was, but the word for "official," *basileos*, indicates that he was a man of authoritative position in the court of king Herod Antipas, ruler of Galilee. Men of such power, either then or now, are not known for having a spirit of humility. Yet this man revealed such a spirit to Jesus and resultantly received grace from the Lord. He demonstrated this humility—this spirit of submissiveness—to Jesus in three ways: through submissively journeying to Jesus, through revealing a genuine (and humble) motivation to Jesus, and through demonstrating an extraordinary faith in Jesus.

He submissively came
the necessary distance to Jesus.

The popularity of Jesus was spreading throughout the region of Galilee at this time because of the miraculous works he was performing. First, Jesus had changed the water into wine at Cana (to where he had now returned); additionally, during his recent trip to Jerusalem we are told that "many people saw the miraculous signs he was doing and believed in his name." It is possible that this official had been in Jerusalem at that time or that he had emissaries there who reported these things about Jesus to him.

If he had been at Jerusalem, he returned to his home in Capernaum to a dire scene: his son was very ill, suffering a fever and at the point of death. Verse 47 informs us of his immediate actions upon hearing of Jesus' return to Galilee: "he went to him and begged him to come and heal his son, who was close to death." This man of position and power personally left his important post to go to Jesus where he was at Cana. Although he certainly could have sent a servant to fetch Jesus, he didn't. This official "begged" Jesus to restore his son only after trekking 25 miles to come to where Jesus was. While Jesus had come to his region, he himself went the necessary distance to connect with Jesus.

There is a lesson in his behavior for us. In a sense, isn't that what we are called to do regarding Jesus in our own lives? John 1:11 describes the incarnation of Christ, with its somewhat disappointing human response, with these words: "he came to that which was his own" (meaning his own "realm"), "but his own" (meaning his own "people") "did not receive him." For persons who want to come to him, salvation in Christ is a two-way street. Christ has done his part in journeying from heaven to be among us—by far he came the greater required distance; but we must also "receive him" by going our own necessary distance to him. We accomplish this by responding to him in the specific ways he has commanded us to: through faith that accepts who he is; thus, believing Jesus' claims and promises; through repentance of sin; through acknowledgment of him to others in our lives; and through submission to him in Christian baptism and subsequently following the continued leading of the Holy Spirit in our lives.

The truth is Jesus has come to you as far as he can come. He can come no further than he has already come. He will come no further than he has already come. What have you done? What are you doing to come to *him*? The royal official serves as an example of one who submissively came the necessary distance to Jesus in order to receive the benefits that Christ could offer. We must be willing to do the same.

He submissively revealed a genuine motivation to Jesus.

When this man begged Jesus to heal his son, the Lord responded with what may be perceived as a criticism. It is important to note, however, as a criticism, it was probably not intended personally to this man; for when Jesus observed, "Unless you people see miraculous signs and wonders...you will never believe" (v. 48), he was speaking about the nation of Israel as a whole at this time. While it is important to note that Jesus did use many miraculous signs to draw people to him and cause them to believe in him, the majority still did not respond to him in faith. Many simply wanted to witness the sensation of a miracle. Thus, his indictment here was directed toward those who possessed a sign-seeking mentality, such as the Jews described in John 2:18 who were demanding "of him, 'What miraculous sign can you show us to prove your authority to do all this?'" Even the royal official's own master, Herod Antipas, is later described as one who "had hoped to see Jesus perform some miracle" (Luke 23:8). Jesus would also critically note of the people of his day that "A wicked and adulterous generation looks for a miraculous sign" (Matthew 16:4).

But this man evidently was not to be lumped into that class of people. He quickly and humbly made it clear that the motivation behind his request to Jesus had nothing to do with witnessing the sensation of a miracle being performed. He had come to Jesus because he was a desperate parent who believed Jesus was the only hope he had to keep his son from dying. (What parent facing a similar circumstance regarding their child cannot relate to him here?) His simple response to Jesus' critique of the people at large is revealed in verse 49: "Sir, come down before my child dies." And

Jesus, knowing the genuineness of his pleading, responded to him in verse 50: "You may go. Your son will live."

While this man's reason for making his request of Jesus was a sincere one, as Jesus implicitly acknowledged it to be, we know that even seemingly desperate requests don't always come with genuine motivations. Consider the following letter that purportedly was written by a "lovesick" woman who had recently broken up with her fiancé. In it she disclosed her latent sorrow for having done so:

> Dearest Jimmy,
>
> No words could ever express the great unhappiness I've felt since breaking our engagement. Please say you will take me back. No one could ever take your place in my heart. Please forgive me. I love you! I love you! I love you!
>
> Yours forever,
> Marie
>
> P.S: And congratulations on winning the lottery.[3]

She obviously didn't have a sincere motive behind her pleadings. Likewise, I believe it is even possible for individuals to come to Jesus for all the wrong reasons. Many people he encountered did come to Jesus with ulterior motives. There were those who came seeking to trap him with disingenuous questions (Matthew 22:15-22; John 8:6). There were throngs who followed him because he had once miraculously filled their bellies with food (John 6:26). Judas once approached him with a kiss—not out of love and respect, but to identify him to his enemies (Matthew 26:48-49). Even today individuals may come to Christ for less than the most ideal of reasons: one may come to him to please someone else in their life; another may come to him out of mere family tradition; still others may come to him—especially in the context of his church—more for purposes

---

[3] Jimmy Botts, *Transforming Love*, sermon at sermoncentral.com.

of social networking than a desire for a changed life. But there was only a genuine and humble motivation in the request of this royal official; Jesus recognized it and responded mercifully to it.

He submissively demonstrated
an extraordinary faith in Jesus.

As the narrative continues in verses 50-53, the subsequent healing of the royal official's son is revealed:

> Jesus replied, "You may go. Your son will live." The man took Jesus at his word and departed. While he was still on his way, his servants met him with the news that his boy was living. When he inquired as to the time when his son got better, they said to him, "The fever left him yesterday about the seventh hour." Then the father realized that this was the exact time at which Jesus had said to him, "Your son will live." So he and all his household believed.

I can't help but think that, were I this man when Jesus told him to "go" and that "your son will live," I would have likely felt great disappointment. While there were claims of Jesus doing some remarkable things, no one had, to this point in the gospel record, given witness to him doing any long-distance miracles. In a later account found in Matthew 8 and Luke 7, Jesus did heal the servant of a centurion, also from Capernaum, from a distance. In this case there was no expectation of a personal appearance by Jesus at the scene. In fact, the centurion even expressed his faith in Jesus to work the requested miracle from any location by insisting,

> Lord, I do not deserve to have you come under my roof. But just say the word, and my servant will be healed. For I myself am a man under authority, with soldiers under me. I tell this one, "Go," and he goes; and that one, "Come," and he comes. I say to my servant, "Do this," and he does it. (Matthew 8:8-9)

42

It is possible that the centurion had heard of this previous healing of his neighbor's son and this knowledge contributed to him possessing such faith. But the royal official had no basis on which to reckon—other than from the mere strength of his faith in Jesus—that our Lord could distantly revive his son. If I were him, I sense that I would have hung my head and insisted that my expectation was for Jesus to come back to Capernaum with me where he could see my son, touch my son, say whatever right words were necessary and heal him. Yet this is not what the royal official did. I love the observation John makes of this man in the last phrase of verse 50: "The man took Jesus at his word and departed."

Wow! What a demonstration of faith! There was no continued pleading; he had no argument with Jesus. There was only simple trust in and obedience to what Jesus had said. What a description of faith! John tells us this man "took Jesus at his word." Isn't that what faith in Christ calls us to do as well—to take Jesus at his word? To believe Jesus' claim that he is the Messiah? (John 4:26). To accept without reservation his claim that "anyone who has seen me has seen the Father?" (John 14:9). To believe without hesitancy his promises that he would go to prepare a place for us and that he will one day return for us? (John 14:1-3.). To practically trust his assurance that "the Father will give you whatever you ask in my name?" (John 15:16).

Believing Jesus' declaration that his son would live, this man "departed." It was one thing for this official to intellectually trust Jesus' claim that his son would be healed; it was another thing to act upon that belief; but he did act upon it by immediately beginning the long journey home, unaccompanied by Christ. He wholly entrusted himself and his situation to Jesus.

John Ortberg supplies the following illustration of this kind of faith—the kind of surrendered faith in Christ that this ruler had, and we are to have as well:

The Flying Roudellas, who were trapeze artists, said there is a special relationship between the flyer and the catcher on the trapeze. The flyer is the one who lets go, and the catcher is the one who catches.

As the flyer swings high above the crowd on the trapeze, the moment comes when he must let go. He arcs out into the air. His job is to remain as still as possible and wait for the strong hands of the catcher to pluck him from the air. The flyer must never try to catch the catcher but must wait in absolute trust. The catcher will catch him, but he must wait.[4]

Like the trapeze flyer, our faith calls us to trust Jesus to do what he says he will do. May we, like the royal official who returned home in full acceptance of Christ's declaration that his son would be healed, practice a trust in him that takes Jesus at his word.

Conclusion

It is somewhat surprising to discover such faith in a man who came from the ranks of the administration of Herod Antipas—a ruler who eventually would be responsible for the beheading of John the Baptist. Yet we learn of others who followed Jesus who shared his background. Joanna was a woman who accompanied Jesus and helped provide for the needs of our Lord and his disciples. She is described as "the wife of Cuza, the manager of Herod's household" (Luke 8:3). According to Acts 13:1, among those Christian leaders in the church at Antioch was "Manaen (who had been brought up with Herod the tetrarch)" (i.e. as a foster brother of Herod Antipas).

It is truly surprising to find such a submissive spirit in one who came from the halls of power, yet this royal official was most humble in his approach to Christ. He demonstrated this by submissively traveling the necessary distance to meet Jesus, by revealing a genuine

---

[4] Craig Brian Larson and Phyllis Ten Elsof, *1001 Illustrations that Connect* (Grand Rapids, MI: Zondervan, 2008), p. 465.

and humble motive to our Lord in his request, and by demonstrating an extraordinary faith by which he, without reticence, simply "took Jesus at his word."

Have you responded to Jesus with his same spirit of submissiveness?

Life Questions

1. Relate an experience in which you have found something in a place where you did not expect to find it? _____

   _____

   _____

   _____

   What was found in an unexpected place in this account? _____

   _____

   _____

2. From your understanding of the doctrine of salvation, what responsibilities do we have in coming to Christ in receiving his offer of salvation? (Preferably cite a verse of Scripture for each responsibility you note.) _____

   _____

   _____

   _____

   _____

3. How did this man exhibit extraordinary faith in Jesus? _____

   _____

   _____

   _____

From your study of the gospels, who else did Jesus meet during his ministry that demonstrated a noteworthy level of faith? _____

_____

_____

4. Who do you know who has what you consider to be extraordinary faith?" _____

_____

_____

5. What claim or promise of Jesus recorded in the Scriptures do you find most difficult to consistently trust in your life? _____

_____

_____

_____

Good News for the Self-Absorbed

—The Lame Man at the Pool—

(John 5:1-15)

Introduction

Of all the types of people that we have considered and will consider in this series, the man at the Pool of Bethesda is perhaps best related to by our current culture. I say this because he appears to be a very self-absorbed man. Self-absorption is defined by the Oxford Dictionary as the practice of being "preoccupied with one's own feelings, interests or situation" (which is often to the exclusion of others or the outside world); it abounds among individuals in our society. With our faces staring into electronic devices we tend to shut out the immediate world around us. Through social media we tend to wear our hearts on our sleeves expressing how we feel about everything and everyone. With the camera lens on our smart phones we call constant attention to ourselves via the "selfies" we take and send to others.

The extreme preoccupation with self that is practiced by some even has a diagnosis: the psychiatric community calls it Narcissistic Personality Disorder (NPD). This is, of course, named after Narcissus, the god from Greek mythology who was cursed by Echo—the young beautiful goddess who was spurned by him—to fall in love with himself. When he came to a pool in the forest and saw his reflection in the water he fell in love with his own image. Not realizing it was himself that he saw, he leaned down to kiss the beautiful creature. One version of the legend says that he fell into the pool and drowned himself.

We've all witnessed people who are narcissistic. I had a friend in school years ago who could never pass a store window when we

47

were walking down the street without stopping to look at himself, often fixing his hair or adjusting his clothes in self-admiration. Indeed, we have all known such individuals.

Of course, you know that narcissism is well-proliferated in our society when it achieves its own changing-a-lightbulb-joke. So, I obligatorily ask, how many narcissists does it take to change a lightbulb? The answer to this? "None—a narcissist would never change a lightbulb; that's a job for the less important people," *or* "One—only he doesn't turn the lightbulb into the socket. He holds it still while the world revolves around him."

Now I'm not suggesting that the lame man in this passage was a full-fledged narcissist (lest you perceive I'm being too harsh), but he was clearly a self-absorbed man. His behavior toward Jesus demonstrated this as we shall see. But Jesus' behavior toward him is even more important to our study of this man. Despite his preoccupation with himself and his situation, Jesus reached out to him in compassion and concern for both his physical and spiritual welfare; and he would not give up on him easily.

The Lame Man's Behavior toward Jesus

He failed to directly answer Jesus' question. Jesus asked a sincere and straightforward question of this man; it may be understood as, "Do you truly desire to get well?" The expected answer was a simple "yes" or "no" (well, really "*yes*"). But the lame man did not offer a direct response. This is much as, in his offer of salvation to us, Jesus essentially asks us if we desire what he is willing to do for us. In this regard, I have observed many who demonstrate an unwillingness to give a "yes" or "no" answer when it comes to the Lord's offer of salvation to them. They hesitate. They procrastinate. They put off any decisive response, sometimes even when it becomes eternally too late for them to respond. But back to the lame man: instead of directly answering Jesus' question...

He focused negatively on his circumstances. As revealed in his response to Jesus in verse 7, the lame man demonstrated a real "woe-is-me" mentality, focusing on the difficulty of his situation: "Sir…I have no man to put me into the pool when the water is stirred up, but while I am coming, another steps down before me." (NASV is used in this chapter). Granted, his was quite a dilemma: healing, he was certain, was available to him if he could only get to the pool when, as verse 4 notes, "an angel…stirred up the water." But he couldn't very well get to the pool if his problem was that he couldn't walk. (The Greek word for "ill" in verse 5, *astheneia*, implies "without strength"—he apparently had none in his legs.) Unlike the paralytic Jesus healed in Mark 2 who was carried to him by four friends and let down through the roof to gain access to the Lord, this man had no such friends or family to assist him by putting him into the water. So, instead of the expected "of course I really want to be healed" in response to Jesus' inquiry, this man chose to dwell on the hopelessness of his situation. And again, I can't help but think of how sometimes that's the same kind of response people give to Christ's offer of salvation in their lives. They focus on the hopelessness of their lives, never believing that the Lord might have a way to conquer their spiritual inadequacy and sense of unworthiness. This man was so zeroed-in on why he could not be healed in the only way he believed he could be healed that he failed to consider any other means for it to happen. He had no sense of what Jesus could do--- which brings me to his next characteristic behavior toward Jesus:

He failed to demonstrate any particular faith in Jesus. Usually when Jesus healed an individual, he did so either upon acknowledgment of their already demonstrated faith (e.g. the Syro-Phoenician woman of Matthew 15) or by commanding an action by which they demonstrated faith (e.g. the ten lepers of Luke 17 who were commanded to "Go and show [them]selves to the priests"). But this man had not admitted to any faith in Jesus, and he was not commanded by Christ to do anything but to "Get up, pick up your pallet and walk." Yet, while he did respond obediently to this directive of our Lord, when you think about it, by the time he did so he was technically already healed!

He focused blame on Jesus. When the man was accused by Jewish religious leaders of breaking the Sabbath by carrying his pallet, he was quite ready to throw Jesus under the bus. Of course, the accusation levied toward him and ricocheted to the Lord was not a legitimate one. The Sabbath regulations of the Jews at this time had much more to do with their interpretations of God's law than the actual regulation God had given. By these interpretations they saw only the letter of the law and not the spirit of it. (It must be noted that Jesus rose above all this by revealing three truths about the Sabbath: [1] that "the Sabbath was made for man" and not the other way around [Mark 2:27-28], [2] that there were reasonable exceptions to the letter of the Sabbath prohibition on labor [Luke 14:5], and [3] that ultimately he as the Son of Man was "Lord of the Sabbath" [Matthew 12:8].) That being noted, I remind you that this man was quite comfortable with passing the buck of blame to Jesus by stating "He who made me well was the one who said to me, 'Pick up your pallet and walk.'" (v. 11). (Do you like this guy yet?)

He failed to thank Jesus for his healing. When he was immediately healed, he quickly chose not to hang around. He was ready to experience his newly granted freedom, so he took off. Just like the nine lepers who did not return to express thanks to Jesus, this man was silent regarding any appreciation toward the Lord. (Note: At least the nine lepers could have used the excuse that they were a distance away from Jesus when they realized their healing and would have had to go back to him; but this man was right in the presence of Christ when he was cured! Yet he said nothing—he didn't even get Jesus' name or ask who he was!) By way of application, in regard to the spiritual healing that we are granted in Christ, our gratitude to him should be expressed verbally and often, and through our everyday living. It must never be neglected or withheld.

He failed to follow Jesus—twice. Instead of pursuing an interest in the One who had, in a moment, made a bigger and greater change in his life than anyone else ever had, he lost Jesus in the crowd. He didn't even seem to know in which direction Jesus went. One is left to wonder how he could allow that to happen! While we are later informed in the text that, at this moment, Jesus "had slipped away" (v. 13) from him, that seems as no excuse to me. Thus, he failed to follow Jesus (which is the very essence of discipleship) when he was healed by him and again, in the end, when Jesus reconnected with him and he had another opportunity to do so. It seems that, like so many people in this world when it comes to Jesus, he was glad to receive the benefits that Christ could provide, but he didn't want to bother with doing what Jesus wanted the man to do for *him*: give Jesus the honor due him for the wonderful healing he had wrought.

Finally, *he failed to defend Jesus.* Once again, when he was then able to identify Jesus, he was quite ready to place the blame on the Lord. While Judas would later identify Jesus to his enemies in the darkness with a kiss, this man identified Jesus to his enemies in the daytime with, as I imagine, a pointed finger (v. 15). Again, I am left to wonder how he could be this way toward Jesus! But then I am reminded of how sometimes I fail to defend Christ to the unbelieving world around me when I feel called upon to do so, and I am convicted that in some ways I am occasionally all-too-much like this man.

Jesus' behavior toward the lame man

Jesus saw him. I believe that it was no accident that Jesus was in this vicinity—just as nothing Jesus ever did was a matter of happenstance. He was there because he knew he would see this man. Maybe he had even seen him there before. And it wasn't that he just physically saw him; he "perceived" him (as indicated by the Greek verb *horao* here). He took note of this man's tragic and desperate condition. Jesus' heart went out to him.

Jesus knew about him. This is one place where I don't prefer the NIV translation which states that Jesus "learned" that he had been there a long time. The original Greek indicates that when Jesus observed him he already knew that this man had been suffering like this for a long time (thus the NASV translates the first part of

51

verse 6, "When Jesus saw him lying there, and knew that he had already been a long time in that condition…"). How did he know? Perhaps because he was God in the flesh and he knew everything about everybody. Perhaps, as already noted, from his human perspective Jesus had previously seen him there on his former journey to Jerusalem. For that matter, this man possibly had been there so long that Jesus may have seen him when he went to the temple when he was 12 years old with Joseph and Mary. He could have been a well-known fixture at these colonnades for decades. Don't misunderstand this circumstance. Jesus didn't have to inquire as to the longevity of this man's suffering; he was already fully cognizant of it—just as he is fully cognizant of all that is going on in our lives.

Jesus chose him. There were all kinds of people with a variety of afflictions at the pool that day whom Jesus did not heal—at least for now. I am content to believe that, while Jesus healed many whom he encountered, there were many who came his way during his earthly ministry whose needs of healing he chose not to meet. My point here is not to address the reasons behind the Lord's selectivity (that's another legitimate subject for another study); my point here is to note how blessed this man was in Jesus' selection of him in this setting.

Jesus challenged him. The Lord implored the lame man as to whether or not he even wanted to get better. Did he truly want a better life than this? It may be hard for us to imagine, but given his lack of a definitive answer to Jesus' inquiry as previously noted, perhaps this man didn't really want to be healed. This was, after all, the only life he had ever known. Was he ready to face the world with the responsibilities that would go with being healthy and whole? As I noted earlier, he never really answered Jesus' question, "Do you want to get well?" Maybe he didn't. On the level of spiritual healing I have discovered this same reality with some people; they don't really want a better life; they're quite comfortable in the familiar sinfulness that disables them.

Jesus elicited obedience from him. He commanded him to "Get up! Pick up your pallet and walk." This is the closest Jesus came to asking for a demonstration of faith from this man. Yet again, by the time he obeyed him he was already healed at the very words of Jesus.

Jesus found him. While this man never appears to look for Jesus after he had lost him in the crowd, Jesus didn't fail to look for him. Verse 14 informs us that "Afterward Jesus found him..." While once Jesus had "slipped away" from him, it becomes clear that Jesus wasn't done with him yet (just as he is never done with us once he has initially spiritually healed us). And it is noteworthy that he finds him "in the temple." For me, this is the most positive thing that John records about this man. After all, if he wasn't at Jesus' feet thanking him, he should have been at the temple sacrificing and praising God for the deliverance he had experienced. (In my optimism I want to believe that's why he was there.) But the point is that Jesus found him there. I sense that Jesus wasn't giving up on this man—just as he tends not to give up on us when our response to him is not all that it should be.

Jesus warned him. When he found the man at the temple Jesus had something curious to say to him: "See, you are well again. Stop sinning or something worse may happen to you." Wow—that's a loaded statement! First, it tells us that Jesus was every bit as concerned—if not more so—about this man's spiritual condition as he was his physical condition. (Are we as equally concerned about this with those around us?) Second, it may imply that, along with healing him, Jesus had also forgiven his sin. You may recall with the paralytic carried by his four friends (Mark 2) that Jesus first pronounced his sins forgiven, then to demonstrate his power to forgive, physically healed him. Jesus had the power on earth to arbitrarily forgive sins and, although not stated, it seems he likely did so with this man. Why would he tell him not to sin anymore if his sins at that moment had not been forgiven? The only other person Jesus said something like this to was the woman caught in adultery in John 8, whom he forgave with the words, "...neither do I condemn you." Then he added, "Go now and leave your life of sin." (John 8:11).

The warning Jesus gave the formerly lame man raises an important issue: "Stop sinning or something worse may happen to you." Something *worse?* One is left to wonder what could be worse than a physical illness that caused one to be unable to walk for 38 years! Yet we know there is something worse than physical suffering. Jesus indicated this when he warned his disciples in Matthew 10:28, "Do not be afraid of those who kill the body but cannot kill the soul. Rather, be afraid of the One who can destroy both soul and body in hell." The ultimate "worse" thing for this man would be to face eternal judgment from God. In fact, this, Jesus appears to be saying here, is the worst thing that can happen to any of us.

F. Furman Kearley once related the story about a rehabilitation counselor who took an early retirement from his profession to spend the rest of his life preaching. One day, while he was addressing an audience, he told of how, early in his career, he came across a young boy with several birth defects. In his capacity he proceeded to arrange medical and financial help for the boy. Subsequently skilled surgeons restored the boy's facial appearance. Then in time trained therapists taught him how to speak and to walk. By the time he reached his teens the young man was able to take part in all the activities of other young people.

Then in his speech he asked his audience: "What do you think has become of this young man?" One hearer guessed that, since the young man had overcome such physical deformities, he may have dedicated himself to becoming a great athlete. Someone else suggested that, since his life had been changed by medical doctors, he had become a skilled surgeon.

"No, none of these," continued the counselor/preacher. "The young man is a prisoner, serving a life sentence for murder. We were able to restore his physical features and his ability to walk and act, but we failed to teach him where to walk and how to act."[5]

Likewise, Jesus enabled the lame man at the Pool of Bethesda to walk; but he also wanted to make sure that this man—self-absorbed as he appears to have been—knew how to walk and where to walk so that he could avoid the "something worse" of God's judgment. He does the same for you and me: he has caused us to be able to spiritually walk. We must constantly reflect as to whether or not we are walking as he has taught us to walk.

Conclusion

As I reflected on Nicodemus earlier in this series of studies regarding this man, I would like to say that this is not the end of his story. I would like to be able to note that he showed up later in John's gospel (as does Nicodemus) or in the book of Acts where he is counted among the disciples. I would like to be able to cite some early church tradition claiming his involvement in laboring alongside one of the apostles as they were taking the gospel to the remotest parts of the earth, thus living his life in thanksgiving to Christ for the healing and forgiveness he had mercifully received. Yet there are no such passages that mention him or traditions that make these claims. What we read in John 5 is all that we know of him. So, the real story here is Jesus' story; for in this account he, consistent with his very purpose, reached out with love to the unlovable; he healed the unappreciative; he forgave without receiving due recognition of it; he refused to give up on someone who didn't seem to have an interest in following him.

When you think about it, doesn't that sound a lot like how Jesus often must be toward you and me?

---

[5] Jeff Strite, *Wonderful Counselor*, sermon at sermoncentral.com

Life Questions

1. What behaviors do you observe among people in our society today that indicate a spirit of self-absorption? _____

   _____

   _____

2. **Thought Question:** Given this man's attitude and behavior toward Jesus, why do you think Jesus healed him? _____

   _____

   _____

3. **Thought Question:** In your opinion, to what do you think Jesus might have been alluding when he warned this man that if he didn't stop sinning, "something worse may happen" to him?_____

   _____

   _____

4. When have you ever sensed that Jesus wasn't giving up on you?

   _____

   _____

   On someone else you know? _____

   _____

   _____

Good News for the Sinner Condemned

—The Adulterous Woman—

(John 8:1-11)

Introduction

I once heard a beloved preacher in our brotherhood of churches, Bob Shannon, relate the story of a church that was affiliated with a denomination of episcopal structure in which the regional bishop appointed the ministers to the congregations within his conference. He appointed an older man to a particular church, and after several months the people of that congregation asked to meet with the bishop to express their displeasure about the minister he had appointed to them. Their complaint was that they didn't like the man because "every Sunday when he preaches he tells us we're going to hell." Acting on their complaint, when it came time a few months later to reappoint ministers, the bishop obliged the congregation by sending the older minister to a different church and replacing him with a younger man.

After several months the congregation asked to meet with the bishop again to register their gripe about this minister. It was the same thing: "The young man you sent us—every week when he preaches he tells us we're going to hell!"

The bishop thought, "Well, they didn't like the young man or the older man—this time I'll send them a middle-aged man." And that's what he did when appointment time came around. The better part of a year went by and the bishop heard nothing from the congregation, so finally he contacted the church's ministry committee to ask how they liked their new minister and they responded that they just loved this guy.

"Well then," the bishop queried, "he must not be preaching that you're going to hell every Sunday."

"No," they replied, "he also tells us we're going to hell every Sunday."

"Then what's the difference?" the bishop asked.

They answered, "Well, when he tells us we're going to hell he says it with a tear in his eyes."

Some people seem to consider it to be their personal calling to be judge and jury in condemning other people of their sin. Most of us have known someone like that in our lives. Perhaps some of us have been that person at times. We know from the gospels that the Pharisees of Jesus' day were like that—and you can bet, from what we know of them, that their actions of condemning others were probably not accompanied by a tear in their eyes. We witness this propensity of the Pharisees, accompanied by their counterparts the scribes, in the account of the adulterous woman in this passage. Perhaps more clearly than anywhere else in the gospels we find them here pursuing the pastime of condemnation. It is evident in these verses that they were quite focused on bringing judgment upon this woman as they brought her to Jesus. But it also becomes clear that their bigger target for condemnation was Jesus himself, for we are informed in verse 6 that the accusers brought the woman to Jesus asking him for his judgment of her situation "as a trap, in order to have a basis for accusing *him*." (emphasis mine)

Yet Jesus had some good news for this woman who was facing a life-threatening circumstance. The good news was the fact that her sin was forgivable and would be forgiven and her accusers would be driven away. As we study this account three important realities surface that we will consider: the first is regarding the *guilt* of the woman, the second is regarding the *guile* of the accusers and the third is regarding the *grace* of Christ that was extended to her.

The guilt of this woman cannot be denied.

Much is made by scholars and translators about the fact that this narrative is not found in any of the early Greek manuscripts of John's Gospel. While it is accepted to be a genuine account from the life of Christ—one which seems to have been handed down in the first several centuries of the church through oral tradition—one reason scholars suggest that it might not have been included was because of the subject matter. It is, after all, a somewhat risque story to be included in sacred writ. This woman was caught in the very act of adultery. Others suggest the omission of this account by Christian scribal copiers was due to Jesus' ready forgiveness of this woman and they didn't want believers to gain the impression that such sexual sin was insignificant or that it was to be condoned among them.

The evidence tells us that this accused woman was truly guilty of committing adultery. That could imply that either participant was married and this was a relationship outside of his or her own marriage, or both were married and it was an extra-marital relationship outside of both of their marriages (Leviticus 20:10; Deuteronomy 22:22), or it was a relationship that was premarital in the case of the woman already being pledged in marriage (Deuteronomy 22:23-24). It is important to note that throughout her ordeal in this passage the woman never attempted to deny the claim of her accusers. By her lack of protesting she appears to own this sin. Neither did Jesus assert that it was not a true indictment; and since Jesus knew the truth about everything, his silence also pointed to the reality of her guilt. Of course, adultery requires the participation of two persons and the absence of the man here is a legitimate concern. While it could be that he was in on the whole charade with the accusers to trap Jesus (which didn't make him any less guilty), still, she had willingly participated in her part of the adultery.

Additionally, it is important that in their accusation they charged this woman with being "caught" in adultery. The necessity of having witnesses to one's being "found sleeping with another man's wife"

59

was essential to pursue the death penalty for this sin according to Deuteronomy 22:22.

I once read about a little boy in Sunday School whose teacher had just finished teaching a lesson on the subject of forgiveness. She wanted to make sure that she had made her point, so she asked the class, "Can anyone tell me what you must do before you can obtain forgiveness for sin?" (Of course, her points had been about repentance and prayer—subjects she was anticipating in the answer.)

The little boy's hand shot up: "Well," he said, "you've got to *sin* first."[6]

The lad might not have been listening to the lesson as well as the teacher had hoped, but his answer was correct. Real sin is a prerequisite to real forgiveness. The woman in this account was genuinely forgiven because she had genuinely sinned. Our forgiveness, too, is based on the reality of our committed sins.

Christian author John Beukema relates the following personal story:

> After moving to a new state, I went to the Department of Motor Vehicles to get a new driver's license. The guy behind the desk said he couldn't help me because my license was suspended.
>
> "There must be some mistake," I said. "I've never done anything to deserve that."
>
> The civil servant was very civil, but said I had to clear up the problem with the State of Massachusetts before he could help me. I hadn't lived in Massachusetts for ten years, so I couldn't imagine what was wrong. Five long-distance phone calls later, I found out that when I moved from Massachusetts, I owed part of an excise tax of $2.

---

[6] Adapted from King Duncan, *Mule Eggs and Topknots* (Knoxville, TN: Seven Worlds Press, 1987), p. 100.

That tiny little bill began to accrue penalties and interest. I had to pay that bill plus the cost of a new Massachusetts driver's license and registration for a car that had long ago become scrap metal before I could become legal in my new home state. The price tag was nearly $300.

The whole thing was embarrassing. It wasn't so much the money that bothered me; it was knowing that I was on the wrong side of the law for all those years.[7]

Realizing that one is, even unwittingly, on the wrong side of the law can be a very sobering experience. The adulterous woman—as we all do---needed forgiveness because she was—as we all are—on the wrong side of *God's* law. In his book *What's So Amazing about Grace?* Philip Yancy writes about this incident in John 8 stating that it illustrates that "People divide into two types: not the guilty and the 'righteous,' as many people think, but rather...guilty people who acknowledge their wrongs and guilty ones who do not."[8] The accused woman seemed to be quite conscious of her guilt; the Pharisees were not so ready to admit theirs. This brings us to the next evident reality from this narrative.

The guile of the accusers is clear to discern.

Earlier in John's gospel, as you may recall, Jesus met a man in whom there was "no guile" (John 1:47 in KJV). The NIV clarifies that there was "nothing false" in Nathaniel. I spoke of Nathaniel as one who was sincere—who had no spirit of deception in him. The opposite may be observed of the Pharisees and scribes who confronted Jesus with this woman. They were innately insincere and deceitful. These accusers were armed with ulterior motives in their actions. Their guile is evident in the things they did.

---

[7] Larson and Ten Elsof, *1001 Illustrations that Connect*, p. 227.
[8] Philip Yancey, *What's So Amazing About Grace* (Grand Rapids, MI: Zondervan, 1997), p. 181.

First, they deceptively cited Scripture. In verse 5 they note— per Leviticus 20:10 and Deuteronomy 22:22—that "In the law Moses commanded us to stone such women." Of course, in citing this directive they conveniently omitted the fact that both of these verses also included the man as a recipient of the death penalty for this sin.

Second, and relative to the above-cited directives of the Law, they did not even accuse the man. Nor did they bring him along, which is curious because, since adultery required the participation of two persons and she had been "caught," wouldn't he also have been caught? Did they simply let him get away? Or was he, via his participation in the adultery, involved with the accusers in the whole plot to find an accusation against Jesus?

Finally, John editorially reveals to us that they were intentionally being deceptive in this scenario. He states in verse 6: "They were using this question as a trap in order to have a basis for accusing him."

The background to this event was that Jesus had come to Jerusalem for the Feast of the Tabernacles. Upon arriving the Lord kept a low profile at first, but then he began drawing crowds to himself as he taught at the temple. When the people began to speculate that Jesus might be the Christ, "the chief priests and Pharisees sent temple guards to arrest him" (John 7:32). The guards had returned empty-handed confessing their wonder regarding Jesus by stating, "No one ever spoke the way this man does" (John 7:46). The animosity against Jesus was dramatically building. The religious leaders were looking for an excuse to kill Jesus, and the way they could accomplish this was to put Jesus in the position of appearing to speak against Roman authority. You see, the Romans at this time did not legally allow the Jews the practice of administering capital punishment. On the other hand, if Jesus would not give the green light to stoning this woman—thus *not* advocating defiance against Rome—they could accuse him of going against the Law of Moses, thus discrediting Jesus with the people.

Witnessing what these accusers were trying to do to Jesus, and Jesus' response to them, brings to my mind a story from American political history:

> Back in 1892, the Vice-Presidential candidate, Adlai Stevenson, grandfather of the former United Nations delegate, was making a railroad whistle-stop tour of the Northwest, where the paramount issue of the campaign was whether the mountain peak which dominates the landscape should be called Tacoma or Rainier.
>
> At some stops the citizens were pro-Rainier; at other stops, pro-Tacoma. It was impossible to avoid the issue. With the aid of the engineer, Stevenson arranged a showmanly device. In every speech he made reference to the beauty of the mountain and referred to the controversy over its name.
>
> "This controversy," he said, "must be settled and settled right by the national government. I pledge myself, here and now, that if elected I will not rest until this glorious mountain is properly named. There is only one appellation which is worthy of consideration, and that is----." Here he pulled the cord which the engineer had installed, whereupon his words were instantly drowned by the scream of the engine whistle as the train pulled out of the station. The sentence was never completed and nobody ever figured out where Stephenson stood on the Tacoma-Rainier controversy.[9]

In the gospels, whether it was being put on the spot about paying taxes to Caesar or the subject of marriage in the resurrection, answering questions regarding from where he got his authority to do the things he did or dealing with the accusation of these accusers, Jesus was not a politician. He never side-stepped issues. He

---

[9] Dick Hyman, *Washington Wind and Wisdom* (Lexington, MA: The Stephen Green Press, 1988), pp. 75-76.

addressed them head on, always got to the real heart of the matter and let the chips fall where they may. Thus, in this account, not only did he address the woman's sin with forgiveness, he also revealed the deceit of her accusers.

The grace of Christ is the cause for deliverance.

The first response from Jesus to the indictment of this woman by the Pharisees and scribes was that of silence. In fact, the King James Version concludes verse 6 with the clarification that "Jesus stooped down, and with his finger wrote on the ground, as though he heard them not." He refused to verbally answer their question. But Jesus' silence didn't dissuade these accusers, for as he was writing in the sand, they persisted in asking for a statement from him about this woman's case.

We must also not overlook Jesus' actions of stooping to the ground and writing in the sand, which he did twice in this passage. The substance of Jesus' writing is often debated among scholars and students of the Scripture. In truth, we do not know what Jesus wrote, although several suggestions have been given: (1) Perhaps Jesus was just "doodling" in the sand as he was thinking about his response. (I've heard this claim argued, but the problem with this is that *katagrapho* implies intelligent scripting; it means literally "to write against;" the *Zondervan NIV Exhaustive Concordance* adds "with a possible implication that what is written is an accusation.") This brings to mind some possible things Jesus might have been writing: (2) Perhaps he wrote down the entirety of the 10 commandments, by which they all would have been reminded of the sins of which they were individually guilty. (3) Perhaps he wrote their individual names with their most common personal sins accompanying them. (This is my personal leaning.) (4) Or perhaps—in the category of the same sin of which they were seeking condemnation of this woman—he wrote the names of women with whom they had participated in sexual dalliances.

Additionally, we must note that between the occasions of writing Jesus did have something to say to these men in verse 7: "If any one of you is without sin, let him be the first to throw a stone at her." Here he asked for judgment from them—not about the woman, but about themselves in reflecting on their own sinful guilt. Again, the KJV, with a basis in some of the rarer manuscripts, adds the clarifying phrase in verse 9: "being convicted by their own conscience." All of this indicates that, whatever Jesus wrote, his words touched the consciences of these accusers. The effect on them was immediate: "Those who heard" (what Jesus had written) "began to go away one at a time, the older ones first..." (v. 9) This is perhaps because the more mature had a more highly-trained sense of discernment and they were quicker to perceive what Jesus was doing as he wrote.

Finally, the saving grace of Christ heroically surfaced in his concluding words to this woman as Jesus asked her about her, now former, accusers:

> Jesus straightened up and asked her, "Woman, where are they? Has no one condemned you?"

> "No one, sir," she replied.

> "Then neither do I condemn you," Jesus declared.
> (vv. 10-11a)

This heretofore condemned sinner had been granted a pardon from the Son of God himself; this was most important because, even though those who had brought her to Jesus could no longer legitimately condemn her, God still could do so, but he extended grace instead. This particular sin—the act of breaking the seventh commandment—would no longer be counted against her. She would now be free from the spiritual penalty of her guilt and the feelings of guilt as well. When you think about it, it's kind of ironic—perhaps even demonstrative of some practical justice—that the man who also participated in the sin but was not brought to Jesus did not receive the blessing of forgiveness.

Lastly, Jesus spoke a command to this woman: "Go now and leave your life of sin." The Greek is more literally rendered, "You go now and do not still be sinning." The present active imperative tense implies the Lord's insistence that this woman should pursue a permanent higher morality for her life. She must use the grace she has received as a motivation to overcome those things that had formerly been temptations to her.

Christian author W. Maynard Pittendreigh relates the following personal experience from his years of working with the South Carolina Department of Corrections:

> ...from time to time, there would be a prison break. It was never as dramatic as it is in the movies. No spotlights beaming from the guard towers, no machine guns, no sirens. We were a minimum-security prison, so we didn't have any of that. So for us a jail break was always low key. The inmates would just disappear and we would find out the next time we counted the inmates and came up short.
>
> The first order of business was always to go to their homes. Almost without fail, that's where they would be. They would just go back to their home and we'd capture them.[10]

Pittendreigh then observes as he applies this experience to us and the woman in this account:

> That's the way it is for all too many of us when we find Christ or experience forgiveness. We tend to go back to the same old place in our lives, doing the same old things, committing the same old sins. Christ doesn't forgive the woman so she can live and commit adultery again. He forgives the woman so she can live and abide by the Law of God.[11]

---

[10] W. Maynard Pittendreigh, *Second Chances*, sermon at sermoncentral.com.
[11] Ibid.

As I like to think of it, Jesus' forgiveness of the woman in John 8 and his concluding command for her to live uprightly reminds us that God's grace in Christ is not to be viewed as an opportunity of license to continue doing what is wrong. Rather, receiving his grace must be a liberating cause for us to pursue what is right.

Conclusion

Jesus offers much more than just a tear in his eye for those who, because of the presence of sin their lives (and that includes all of us), were destined for hell. He offers intervention to forego the consequences of sin. He stands between us and our accusers —not only our would-be earthly accusers, but namely our most formidable accuser (the one whose very title means "accuser"), Satan. He demonstrated his power to do so in this account of a woman who was genuinely guilty of the sin with which she was charged, whose accusers were clearly and hypocritically deceitful, yet who was delivered dramatically by the grace of Christ. In many ways her story is the story of every redeemed child of God.

Life Questions

1. What is the difference, if any, between legitimately confronting someone regarding their sin and what the accusers of the woman did in this passage? _____

   _____

   _____

   _____

2. How did the Pharisees misrepresent Scripture to Jesus in their accusation of this woman? _____

   _____

   _____

Have you ever heard anyone try to misquote or misrepresent Scripture to interpret its message for their own advantage? _____ If so, with what passage did they do this and how were they misusing it? _____

_____

3. In your opinion, what do you think Jesus wrote in the sand? Was it one of the possibilities cited, or would you offer another suggestion?_____

_____

_____

4. **Thought Question:** Why do you think Jesus chose to forgive the woman caught in adultery? _____

_____

_____

_____

Good News for the Sightless

—The Man Born Blind—

(John 9:1-41)

Introduction

I once heard about a woman who was standing on a street corner waiting to cross a busy thoroughfare. Suddenly a man stood beside her and held out his arm. The woman, surprised at his chivalrous gesture, gladly and trustingly took the man's arm and began traversing across the street with him. As soon as they started across cars began honking, vehicles were swerving, tires were screeching and drivers began yelling some not-too-nice things out of their car windows. The couple almost got hit several times.

When they finally made it to the other side, they were quite disheveled from all of their close calls. The woman was irate: "You almost got us killed—you idiot! I trusted you to take me across the street and you led us right out into oncoming traffic!" She continued, "What were you trying to do—are you blind or something?"

"Why yes, ma'am; I *am* blind," the man responded. "That's why I held out my arm to get some assistance in crossing the street."

Stated ironically, sightlessness is not always easily seen. John 9 relates the story of Jesus' encounter with a man who had been born blind. It reveals to us another wonderful and miraculous healing episode from John's gospel pointing us to the truth that Jesus is the Son of God. Yet, as I study this narrative, I am impressed with the fact that this man who was physically blind appears to be not the only person in this account who experienced some blindness; there are others in this narrative who exhibited it as well. Among them are the disciples and the Jewish religious leaders who demonstrated their own forms of lacking sight. Even the man who was physically blind—as we shall see—had another level of blindness to overcome once he had received healing from physical sightlessness.

The Reason for this Man's Suffering

As Jesus and his disciples were leaving the temple area where the Lord had been teaching and experiencing confrontation with the Jewish religious leaders, they saw a man who was blind. The fact that they immediately knew this man was sightless from the day he was born tells us that he was—perhaps as formerly in the case of the lame man at the pool—a familiar sight to them. His blindness from birth also raised a question in the minds of Jesus' disciples: since this man entered the world suffering in this way, then what was the cause of it?

The popular view among the Jews at the time was that such suffering was the result of God's retribution for someone's personal sin. The disciples reflected this view in the question they presented to Jesus. They did not ask whether or not it *was* sin that led to this man's suffering; they inquired presumptively *whose* sin was being judged through it: "Who sinned," they asked, "this man or his parents that he was born blind?" (v. 2). Logically, it seems to me, the expected answer from the Lord would have been that it was a sin of the parents that had caused it. Since the sightlessness had been from the man's birth, blame toward him would have required him to have sinned before he was even born.

In his response to the disciples Jesus made it clear that they were thinking incorrectly about the cause of this blindness being connected to a singular sin—or even that it was the result of God's judgment at all. Considering their question, it may be fair to infer that the disciples were demonstrating some blindness of their own at this point. Theirs was not realized in a physical lack of sight; theirs was a blindness about the nature of evil and suffering. They assumed, per the view of their day, that this man's suffering resulted from divine retribution for someone's specific sin. To them it was as though God practiced a kind of *quid pro quo* where sinful behavior and suffering was concerned. But Jesus made it clear that there is a larger picture to be seen in the cause of individual suffering. In this case, which may have possessed some uniqueness to it, this man's

70

suffering was for the ultimate end of his experiencing "the work of God…displayed in his life." (v. 3)

Of course, by pointing this out Jesus was not declaring there is no connection between sin and suffering, but he was denying the this-for-that model of it assumed by the disciples—especially where the role of God in suffering is concerned. Practically speaking (and biblically speaking) we know that suffering can result from sin via a cause-effect relationship. In biblical language this occurs when one "reaps what one sows" from sinful activity (Proverbs 22:8; Galatians 6:7). This principle is recognized in our axiom "if you play with fire you can get burned."

Yet, there is even a larger connection between sin and suffering than this. The very reality of suffering exists because of the presence of sin in this "fallen" world. On the immediate level this is seen in the fact that when sin was introduced into the world by the partaking of the forbidden fruit in the Garden of Eden, both Adam and Eve resultantly experienced their own forms of suffering. For Adam the ground was "cursed" and he could only reap from its benefits through "painful toil;" for Eve the pains of childbearing and childbirth were greatly increased (Genesis 3:16-19). All suffering that followed from that moment—even death itself—may be traced back to that introduction of sin into the earthly realm. Yet, while there are certainly these connections between sin and suffering, the presumption that any specific incident of suffering indicates divine judgment on an individual sin is not ours to make.

This is a truth that Jesus taught consistently. In a positive sense he revealed that God "causes his sun to rise on the evil and the good, and sends rain on the just and unjust" (Matthew 5:45). If God practiced a *quid pro quo* system this would not happen. Jesus addressed this same truth from a negative perspective in Luke 13:1-5. When he was informed of an incident in which Pilate had killed certain Galileans and mixed their blood with their sacrifices, Jesus addressed the wrongful assumption that their suffering was indicative of some specific and horrible sin they had committed:

Jesus answered, "Do you think that these Galileans were worse sinners than all the other Galileans because they suffered this way? I tell you, no! But unless you repent, you too will all perish."

Then Jesus cited another catastrophic incident from the news of his day to make the same point (only here the suffering seems to have been more random than in the former case):

Or those eighteen who died when the tower in Siloam fell on them—do you think they were more guilty than all the others living in Jerusalem? I tell you, no! But unless you repent, you too will all perish.

In these verses our Lord teaches that sin causes suffering for all of us, but not necessarily in a one-to-one sense. In fact, physical suffering in this world can often be quite random. In a sense he is warning his hearers that "this could happen to you, too," while offering the resolution that the only way suffering can ultimately be overcome is through repentance of all sin and wholly turning to God.

Jesus did, however, answer the disciples' question—sort of. In his answer he suggested, as previously indicated, some uniqueness to this man's circumstance. This man's blindness had an aim to it in that "it happened so that the work of God may be displayed in his life" (v. 3). While addressing this as the purpose of the man's blindness, it is fair to note that Jesus still didn't reveal the innate *cause* of his suffering. It is tempting to infer here, since God had a purpose in this man's suffering, that God himself had caused it to happen. Please note that Jesus did not say that. This man's suffering could just as well have been the result of a random reality in a fallen world. As well, it could have been the result of a personal attack of Satan upon this man (remember Job?) even from the innocence of birth. Jesus' point was that, whatever was the original cause of suffering, God would demonstrate his ultimate power over the evil that caused it through healing him. And that's exactly what he did.

The bottom line for us and the disciples is this: when it comes to discerning the specific cause for suffering in any individual circumstance, we often cannot know with certainty what is that cause. The ready tendency to which many people are prone is to blame God first in some way for the presence of suffering. Even the disciples did this here by intimating their belief regarding suffering as divine retribution. Whenever we do that, it seems to me we may fail to give the Devil his due. Satan is the ultimate source of evil and the father of suffering. God alone—as this incident serves to remind us—is able to conquer the effects of evil that we experience. I like the insight Marlin Vis offers on this matter as he writes,

> Don't blame God for cancer, diabetes, AIDS, malformed babies, or any other disease or malady that afflicts humankind. They weren't a part of God's created order. They came along with humankind's fall. God hates them as much as we do. God works along with us to defeat them. On occasions he chose to reveal his power through a healing miracle but those were always the exception and never the rule, a ray of hope for the hopeless, a promise of healing to come for all people.[1]

The Reality of this Man's Healing

John 9:6-7 describes Jesus' healing of this man:

> Having said this, he spit on the ground, made some mud with the saliva, and put it on the man's eyes. "Go," he told him, "wash in the Pool of Siloam" (this word means "sent"). So, the man went and washed and came home seeing.

The genuineness of the blind man's healing was attested to by several witnesses; these included the man's neighbors and passersby who had seen him begging, the man himself and his parents. Their witness regarding the healing is the subject of a great portion of this chapter, as found in verses 8-23.

---

[1] Marlin Viz, *The Blame Game*, published sermon by *Preaching Today*.

Regarding the testimony of the neighbors/passersby there was some division. Some of them were quite ready to believe, recognizing him without a doubt as the man they knew as the blind beggar. Others were 'blinded' by the tendency to doubt, insisting that this was not the man; it was only someone (who could see) who merely looked like their neighbor. (Of course, when you think about it, it is quite likely that the physical appearance of this man to his neighbors and other observers had changed to a degree with his healing. Certainly, the identifying factor of his eyes was different. He now had eyes with which he could look back at them.)

When the man insisted that he was the man and testified that Jesus had healed him in the way that he did, he admitted that he did not know where Jesus could then be found. Of course, since he was still blind when he had been in the presence of Jesus, it is logical to conclude that this man had never physically seen Jesus. Thus, he likely could not have pointed him out to anyone as his healer, anyway.

Subsequently the neighbors took the man to the Pharisees. When they were confronted with the man's testimony to Jesus' healing of him their primary concern did not turn to the genuineness of the miracle, but to the fact that it had been performed on the Sabbath day. For them, even the activity of making mud on the Sabbath would have gone against the prohibition to labor on that day. They concluded that Jesus' disregard of the Sabbath law branded him a sinner and, ironically, such a sinner could not be used of God to perform miracles. Yet, even within the ranks of the Pharisees there was division over this matter at this point (v. 16).

The man was insistent and consistent in the account of his healing, and he professed to the Pharisees that he believed Jesus to be "a prophet" (v. 17). The general disbelief of the Pharisees is noted in verse 18: "The Jews still did not believe that he had been blind and had received his sight..." Their response at this point indicated a willing spiritual blindness regarding Jesus on behalf of these religious leaders.

The final, and most convincing source of testimony to this man's healing came from the man's own parents. They were summoned by the Pharisees and wholly corroborated the background story to them: "We know he is our son...and we know he was born blind..." (v. 20), but they

74

pled ignorance as to the logistics of his healing since they were apparently not present when the miracle wrought by Jesus occurred. Yet, even the testimony of the parents did not convince the Pharisees that Jesus had genuinely performed this miracle. Despite this powerful witness, they persisted in their disbelief regarding it as well as their insistence that Jesus was "a sinner."

As I consider the unwillingness of the Pharisees to acknowledge this miracle at this point, I am reminded of the following story by Harold Bermel that appeared in *The Christian Reader*:

> We were driving through Pennsylvania Dutch Country with my daughter and her seven-year-old son. We passed an Amish horse and buggy, and my grandson's curiosity was stirred.
>
> "Why do they use horses instead of automobiles?" My daughter explained that the Amish didn't believe in automobiles.
>
> After a few moments, he asked: "But can't they see them?"[2]

As I study this account, I find myself wanting to say to these religious leaders: "The very Son of God is right in your midst doing all of these wonderful things that prove his identity! Can't you *see* him?" I often feel that same sentiment toward those today who continue not to accept Jesus for who he was and is, choosing to remain in their unbelief despite the myriad of witnesses in the Scriptures and beyond them to his claims. If you are such a person, I appeal to you that you not allow such spiritual blindness toward Jesus to eternally overtake you.

The Reasoned Testimony This Man Offered

So, the parents of the formerly blind man insisted that the Pharisees once again should ask their son, who was "of age," to supply for them the details of his healing. Again, they sent for him. Verses 24-34 record the entirety of the second conversation they had with this man. The intent

---

[2] Edward K. Rowell, Ed., *Humor for Preaching and Teaching* (Grand Rapids, MI: Baker Books, 1996), p. 69.

of the Pharisees throughout the dialogue was to pressure the man into not giving Jesus the credit for his healing. Yet at every point the man remained firm in his claim that it was Jesus who had healed him. While he didn't argue that Jesus was the Christ (he had not yet been introduced to this truth about Jesus), he did defend the Lord powerfully to them as the worker of his miracle.

It must be noted that in his first interview with the Pharisees this man had already expressed that he believed Jesus to be "a prophet" (v. 17); in response to this second inquiry, the healed man beautifully defended Jesus simply on the basis of the results that were realized in his own life because of what Jesus had done. I love his response in verse 25 to the Pharisee's renewed declaration that Jesus was "a sinner:" "He replied, 'Whether he is a sinner or not, I do not know. One thing I *do* know. *I was blind but now I see.*'" (emphasis mine)

I assure you that I strongly believe in the study and use of apologetics when it comes to defending the Christian faith. I am confident that—in the marketplace of ideas—whether one is arguing philosophically, scientifically or historically for the claims of Christianity that our faith, when properly presented, can more than hold its own over all other belief systems in the debate arena: when it comes to the physical world, the model of creation wins logically over evolutionary models; the answers of Christianity to the problems of evil and suffering are absolutely more satisfactory than those offered by any other belief system; and the historic claims of and about Jesus are attested to as much as (and often more than) any event from antiquity. I firmly believe that we should argue for our faith along these lines, and in doing so I am confident that we can convince many people of the truths of the Christian faith. But do you know how we can convince even more people about Jesus—especially in this post-modern era in which so many rules for reasoning have been tossed aside? We can do so by simply talking to them about what Jesus has done for us—just like the formerly blind man did!

In his book *A Severe Mercy* Sheldon Vanauken puts it this way: "The best argument for Christianity is Christians: their joy, their certainty, their completeness."[3] This is quaintly illustrated in the following story once related in the monthly devotional *Our Daily Bread*:

> Sociology professor Anthony Campolo recalls a deeply moving incident that happened in a Christian junior high camp where he served. One of the campers, a boy with spastic paralysis, was the object of heartless ridicule. When he would ask a question, the boys would deliberately answer in a halting, mimicking way.
>
> One night his cabin group chose him to lead the devotions before the entire camp. It was one more effort to have some "fun" at his expense. Unashamedly the spastic boy stood up, and in his strained, slurred manner—each word coming with enormous effort—he said simply, "Jesus loves me—and I love Jesus!" That was all. Conviction fell upon those junior-highers. Many began to cry. Revival gripped the camp. Years afterward, Campolo still meets men in the ministry who came to Christ because of that testimony.[4]

Let it be noted that, in response to the man's statement in verse 25, the Pharisees did not seem to know how to answer him. They reverted to asking him about the details of his healing, as revealed in verses 26-27:

> "What did he do to you? How did he open your eyes?"
>
> He answered, "I have told you already and you did not listen. Why do you want to hear it again? Do you want to become his disciples, too?"

That last inquiry of the healed man was more than they could take, as their final conversation with him indicates in verses 28-33:

> Then they hurled insults at him and said, "You are this fellow's disciple! We are disciples of Moses! We know that God spoke

---

[3] Sheldon Vanauken, *A Severe Mercy* (New York: Harper and Rowe, 1977), p. 85.
[4] *Our Daily Bread* (Grand Rapids, MI: RBC Ministries, April 1, 1993)

to Moses, but as for this fellow, we don't even know where he comes from."

The man answered, "Now that is remarkable! You don't know where he comes from, yet he opened my eyes. We know that God does not listen to sinners. He listens to the godly man who does his will. Nobody has ever heard of opening the eyes of a man born blind. If this man were not from God, he could do nothing."

The final frustration of the Pharisees is revealed in verse 34: "To this they replied, 'You were steeped in sin at birth; how dare you lecture us!' And they threw him out."

That last statement indicates that they made good with this man on their previously declared warning that "anyone who acknowledged that Jesus was the Christ would be put out of the synagogue" (v. 22). The price for his claimed belief that Jesus was "from God" was excommunication from the Jewish religious community; and while he still wasn't fully informed as to Jesus' complete identity, his experience with Jesus made him willing to pay that price.

At this point I feel convicted by this man's story as I reflect upon the following thought: does my experience with Jesus—as well as my fuller knowledge of his identity—make me willing to pay any price that may be demanded of me due to my testimony about him? Whether it is isolation from community, the rejection and/or ridicule of family and friends, suffering financial hardship or legal repercussions, would I be willing to pay that price by not backing down where Jesus is concerned? Would you? Like this man, may we relate with the Psalmist who declared, "Come and listen, all you who fear God, and I will tell you what he did for me" (Psalm 66:16)—no matter what the price may be.

The Real Need this Man Had

The final verses of this chapter relate how Jesus found the man he had healed and spoke to him of the most important need that he had in his life—one even greater than overcoming physical blindness from birth. Notice their conversation in verses 35-38:

> Jesus heard that they had thrown him out, and when he found him, he said, "Do you believe in the Son of Man?"
>
> "Who is he, sir?" the man asked. "Tell me so that I may believe in him."
>
> Jesus said, "You have now seen him; in fact, he is the one speaking with you."
>
> Then the man said, "Lord, I believe," and he worshiped him.

Jesus had miraculously helped this man overcome a great struggle in his life by ridding him of physical blindness; and it was good that Jesus, by his power as God in the flesh, rid him of the suffering he had experienced from birth. But Jesus wasn't done with this man yet because he knew of his greater need. Much like Jesus later found the lame man he had healed at the pool, the Lord also sought this man out among the crowded Jerusalem streets, and he found him. And much as he had warned the lame man to "stop sinning, or something worse may happen to you," he also addressed the spiritual issues at stake in this man's life.

Specifically, his need was to "believe"—now and for a lifetime—in Jesus as "the Son of Man" (a messianic title based on Daniel 7:13-14). While this man had already claimed belief in the *power* of Jesus, now, in order to realize the greater, saving spiritual benefits of Christ, he needed to believe in the *person* of Jesus whom he had "now seen" (literally) for the first time. To his credit the man did not hesitate with his confession of faith in and subsequent worship of Christ (v. 38).

The well-known infomercial guru and erstwhile pop-psychologist, Tony Robbins, has come up with what he calls the Six Human Needs. They are as follows:

6. Contribution—We have need to make the world a better place and add value to the world around us.

5. Growth—We have need to become better as a person, to improve our skills, learn, stretch and excel in our lives.

4. Love—We want to be cared about, loved, feel a part of someone's life and have a meaningful connection to them.

3. Significance—We want to feel that our lives have meaning and we have value.

2. Variety—We have need of unexpected events that add adventure to our lives.

1. Comfort—We all want comfort in our lives—the certainty that things will happen in a certain way.[5]

While I don't disagree that any of the above-cited human needs are genuine, I am impressed with the fact that Robbin's list overlooks what is truly the greatest need that any human being has: the need to be at peace with God. Jesus consistently taught this to be our greatest need. In the case of the healed lame man Jesus had made it clear that his most important need—one even greater than overcoming the inability to walk for 38 years—was to "stop sinning or something worse may happen" to him. Likewise, Jesus sought out this formerly blind man to instruct him as to his greater need—one that was even more urgent than overcoming a lifetime of physical blindness---which was to "believe in the Son of Man," who is the means of realizing peace with God. Additionally, Jesus taught that with the realized pursuit of this highest need we experience satisfaction in all of our other areas of need; for this is what he meant when he declared in Matthew 6:33, "But seek first his kingdom and his righteousness, and all these things will be given to you as well."

So much of the focus of our lives is given to pursuing "all these things" while sadly many neglect the most important thing. Even as Christians, in our concerns for others, we may find ourselves spending so much time, effort and energy ministering to—even praying for—physical, psychological and social needs that we fail to prioritize in our message the

[5] Summarized from Tony Robbins, "6 Basic Needs That Make Us Tick," article at entrepreneur.com, December 4, 2014. These seem to be based on Abraham Maslow's Hierarchy of Human Needs.

need for people to be right with God. Jesus didn't neglect this and we must not either.

Conclusion

I once read about a woman named Rose Crawford who had been blind for 50 years. Medical research had advanced to the point that surgery could be done that would deal with the problem of her particular type of blindness. She successfully had this surgery. Consider her experience as she saw for the first time:

> "I just can't believe it!" she gasped as the doctor lifted the bandages from her eyes after her recovery from delicate surgery in an Ontario hospital. She wept for joy when for the first time in her life a dazzling and beautiful world of form and color greeted eyes that were now able to see.[6]

What a beautiful account of physical healing! But here's the bittersweet side to her experience:

> The amazing thing about the story, however, is that 20 years of her blindness had been unnecessary. She didn't know that surgical techniques had been developed, and that an operation could have restored her vision at the age of 30. The doctor said, "She just figured there was nothing that could be done about her condition." Much of her life could have been very different.[7]

I am convinced that many people are like her when it comes to the experience of spiritual blindness. They are simply not aware of the solution—the healing—that is already at hand and readily available to them. If this describes you, please be assured that Jesus has made such healing accessible to you. He demonstrated his ability to do so through the granting of sight to the man who had been born blind. The reason he

---

[6] Mark Shaufele, *A Messiah You Can Believe In*, sermon at sermoncentral.com.
[7] Ibid.

had been born blind we ultimately do not know. We only know that God used his blindness and subsequent healing to glorify himself and testify to his Son. The reality of his healing was undeniable—witnessed to by the man himself, his neighbors and even his parents. The reasoned testimony of this man to the unbelieving Pharisees was a most powerful one: "I was blind but now I see!" And while the story of his physical healing made an inestimable difference in his life, the most important need he had (that was also met by Jesus) was spiritual. What Jesus could do for this need would make an even greater difference in this man's life and in his eternity.

Life Questions

1. Do you think the *quid pro quo* (this for that) concept of God's judgment for sin is still believed by people today? _____ How would you respond to someone who claims to believe this? _____
   _____

2. Who in this account, other than the man who experienced physical blindness, also experience some kind of "blindness," and what kind of blindness did they experience? _____
   _____
   _____

3. Do you agree that the greatest human need is to be at peace with God? _____ Why or why not? _____
   _____
   _____

4. As a Christian, what would your testimony be to someone who asked what Jesus has done for you? _____
   _____
   _____

Good News for the Sufferers of Death

—Martha, Mary, and Lazarus—

(John 11:1-44)

Introduction

Lazarus and his sisters, Martha and Mary, were friends of Jesus. He had visited their home in Bethany (just outside of Jerusalem) on an earlier journey to Judea as recorded in Luke 10:38-41. It is likely that it was at their home that Jesus stayed during the passion week since Matthew 21:17 informs us that Jesus spent the nights at Bethany during that week. The apostle John tells us in John 11:2 that Mary is the one who later anointed Jesus with an expensive vial of perfume (John 12:1-7). This family was dear to Jesus. Lazarus was described to Jesus, in the report of his illness to him, as "the one you love" (v. 3). John 11:5 states that "Jesus loved Martha and her sister and Lazarus." While Jesus loved (and loves) everyone, the text makes it clear that these folks were special to him. Yet, just because they were close friends of Jesus didn't mean that they were exempt from bad things happening to them. (It never means that.) Even calamitous death would encroach upon this faithful family, preceded by a somber illness.

I entitle this lesson "Good News for the Sufferers of Death." This reference is inclusive of Mary, Martha and Lazarus; for while it was Lazarus who physically suffered death (as well as the illness that was prelude to it), his sisters also suffered death in experiencing the pain of bereavement in the face of their brother's untimely passing.

When Lazarus became ill, the sisters sent word of his friend's suffering to Jesus. The Lord was across the Jordan in the region of Perea at this time because of the threat of death from the religious leaders in Judea. When he received word of Lazarus' dire circumstance there, he chose to remain in that region for two additional days before he began the journey toward Bethany.

Now I am confident that, upon hearing about Lazarus, Jesus could have simply spoken the word from where he was and healed his friend in long-distance fashion as he did in the case of the royal official's son in John 4, but he chose not to do this. After the two days in Perea, Jesus had an interesting conversation with his disciples in which he insisted to them that it was then time for them to go back to Jerusalem. His disciples sensed this would mean death for him (and possibly them), but they agreed to go anyway. In Jesus' expressed determination to return to Jerusalem he brought up the situation with Lazarus:

> ...he went on to tell them, "Our friend Lazarus has fallen asleep; but I am going there to wake him up."
>
> His disciples replied, "Lord, if he sleeps, he will get better." Jesus had been speaking of his death, but his disciples thought he meant natural sleep.
>
> So then he told them plainly, "Lazarus is dead, and for your sake I am glad I was not there, so that you may believe. But let us go to him." (John 11:11-15)

Jesus and his disciples commenced traveling toward Jerusalem, arriving in Bethany two days later. When they came upon the home of Lazarus and his sisters, they found many friends gathered to comfort Mary and Martha in the wake of their brother's death. Martha heard Jesus was near and went out to meet him. In her conversation with Jesus she indicated the faith she had in him, first declaring, "Lord...if you had been here, my brother would not have died," followed by her expressed confidence that "I know that even now God will give you whatever you ask." (vv.20-21)

Jesus responded to her with the good news, "Your brother will rise again" (v. 23). Martha interpreted this promise in connection with the final resurrection which Jesus had earlier taught (see John 5:28-29;

6:39-40); but Jesus, who is "the resurrection and the life" had something more immediate in mind.

Martha then sent word of Jesus' arrival to her sister Mary who got up quickly and came to Jesus, falling at his feet (the very feet she would soon anoint). She repeated the same expression of faith that Martha had earlier stated: "Lord, if you had been here, my brother would not have died" (v. 32). When she said this, she did so through tears. Jesus was so moved by the crying of Mary and the mourners who were present that he himself famously "wept." Those with Mary and Martha were impressed by Jesus' evident love for Lazarus, but they were confused as to why—miracle worker that he was—Jesus didn't stop his dear friend from dying (v. 37). At this point Jesus went to the tomb and commanded that the stone be removed. Martha responded to this directive by expressing consternation about the stench of the body after four days in the tomb. Jesus insisted to her, "Did I not tell you that if you believed, you would see the glory of God." Jesus' intent all along had been to dramatically raise Lazarus from the dead.

Jesus arrived amidst very dire circumstances. Death had won, defeating this godly family, but Jesus brought good news regarding death because of his ability to conquer even this formidable foe. This good news was certainly for Mary, Martha and Lazarus, yet it was also for the disciples who witnessed Lazarus' miraculous return to life. The good news of death's defeat, demonstrated in the power of Christ in this account, remains a central tenet to the gospel which is believed and proclaimed by those who are friends of Jesus today. Consider the following truths that surface about death from this account:

The perception of death was changed by Jesus.

Two days after receiving the report of Lazarus' illness Jesus determined to go to Judea. He had already told the disciples that "this sickness will not end in death" (v. 4) for his friend; yet in stating this Jesus already knew that Lazarus was physically deceased (v. 14). It is noteworthy how Jesus spoke to his disciples about the reality of Lazarus' demise in verse 11: "Our friend Lazarus has fallen asleep." "Sleep" was often used to speak of death in the bible. Yet this language is generally referenced differently in the Old Testament when compared with its use in the New Testament. Most commonly in the Old Testament it was used to describe the deaths of various individuals—most often kings who came to the end of their lives—with the phrase "[he] slept with his fathers" (e.g. 1 Kings 2:10;11:43; 14:20; 22:50; 2 Kings 20:21; 21:18 [NASV]) In a more cynical context Job used "sleep" as a metaphor for death to signify the finality of its occasion, offering virtually nothing of hope beyond it:

> But man dies and is laid low;
>   he breathes his last and is no more.
> As waters disappear from the sea
>   or a riverbed becomes parched and dry,
> so man lies down and does not rise;
>   till the heavens are no more, men will not awake
>   or be aroused from their sleep. (Job 14:10-12)

Only in the book of Daniel in the Old Testament do we find the "sleep" of death cited in the context of a message regarding the hope (and judgment) that lies beyond it: "Multitudes who sleep in the dust of the earth will awake: some to everlasting life, others to shame and everlasting contempt." (Daniel 12:2). It is with this same understanding that Jesus spoke of death in terms of "sleep" in John 11; for as he did so he was emphasizing the temporary nature of death since sleep, as we experience it in life, is a temporary thing.

This isn't the only time in the gospels that Jesus referred to someone's physical death as merely "sleep." At the deathbed of Jairus' daughter he declared the girl not to be dead, but just "asleep," only to be laughed at by those surrounding her who knew that she had indeed died (Matthew 9:24; Luke 8:52-53). Why would Jesus do this? Because he intended to bring a change to the human perception of death. Because of what he would eventually accomplish through his own resurrection, death would no longer be understood to be a permanent state for humankind. Like physical sleep from which we awaken, death will be a temporary reality through which we will pass until the resurrection.

In later New Testament writings the apostle Paul underscored this doctrine for Christians. In 1 Thessalonians 4:13-15 he wrote of those who had died in the Lord as those who have "fallen asleep in him." He used the same language regarding those who have died in the Lord in 1 Corinthians 15:6,20, in the latter verse expressing that "Christ has indeed been raised from the dead, the firstfruits of those who have fallen asleep."

I recently read the following information about Blackbeard, the infamous pirate:

> Blackbeard had a ruthless reputation, no doubt, but there was more to him than met the eye. Blackbeard cultivated an image of intimidation with his big tricorn hat and numerous swords, knives, and firearms. He went so far as to weave hemp and lit matches to his beard, resulting in a smoke cloud that made him "look like the devil," according to observers.
>
> But the image Blackbeard was so careful to maintain did not do justice to his true character. In fact, he was shrewd but surprisingly merciful, and there are no verified sources that suggest he ever killed anyone personally. With a reputation that preceded him, perhaps he never felt the need.[8]

Like Blackbeard, death has a ruthless reputation. Jesus, by changing the perception that we have of death as only he who would ultimately overcome death could, has clearly and intentionally mitigated that reputation. For those who by faith look to him, the fearful state of death is understood as a mere "sleep."

---

[8] Jim Kraus, Publisher, *Fascinating Information Pastors Gotta Know* (Carol Stream, IL: Tyndale House Publishing, May 2018).

The pain of death is consoled by Jesus.

There is real pain in death. Often physical death is accompanied by physical pain for the one who is dying. I remember hearing my father say on more than one occasion, "As a Christian I'm not afraid to die—I just don't like the idea of going through the process." I would like to say that when he did pass from this life he was exempted from any discomfort accompanying the experience, but that would misrepresent his reality. Few there are who go through little to no pain in death's process; we may consider such persons—especially when they are Christians who are prepared for death—as blessed.

It is reasonable to assume that Lazarus experienced pain in death. Four times the text tells us that he was "sick" (the Greek verb *astheneo* implying a weakened condition). While the length of his suffering seems to have been limited to just a few days, it is also important to note that Jesus did not stop or lessen the pain of this illness for Lazarus. (We have no promise that he will for us, either.) Yet, while we may go through such suffering at the threshold of entering eternity, Christ's doctrine of the momentary nature of death along with the biblical promise of a glorious resurrection helps to make even this bearable.

It may be fairly observed that the apostle Paul was suffering a slow death throughout his life of service to the Lord. Indeed, the discussion of his personal and chronic suffering is a major theme of his second epistle to the Corinthians as he defended the legitimacy of his apostleship. In 2 Corinthians 4:16-5:2, Paul compared our suffering that ultimately culminates in death to the glory of our heavenly existence that is ushered in by death:

> Therefore we do not lose heart. Though outwardly we are
> wasting away, yet inwardly we are being renewed day by day.
> For our light and momentary troubles are achieving for us an
> eternal glory that far outweighs them all. So we fix our eyes
> not on what is seen, but on what is unseen. For what is seen
> is temporary, but what is unseen is eternal. Now we know
> that if the earthly tent we live in is destroyed, we have a
> building from God, an eternal house in heaven, not built by

human hands. Meanwhile we groan, longing to be clothed with our heavenly dwelling....

Yet, as we witness in John 11, the comfort Christ offered in the face of death went beyond his promise of a glorious eternity on the other side of it. His comfort was also extended to the bereaving. The presence of Christ was crucial in this account. The sisters both professed their sense of the importance of Jesus' presence in their identical declarations, "Lord, if you had been here, my brother would not have died" (vv. 21 and 32). They were likely correct in this observation. It is apparent that this is why Jesus chose to keep his distance for two additional days—to let his friend actually die (vv. 14-15).

Jesus hadn't been there, and Lazarus was now deceased and had been in the grave for four days. In this circumstance the comfort Christ offered was for the sorrowing sisters and their accompanying mourners. Verse 35—the shortest verse in all of the Scripture—familiarly informs us "Jesus wept." Scholars offer various explanations as to why Jesus shed tears at this moment. Some suggest the cause to be that of his own personal bereavement at the passing of his friend. (The problem with this is that Jesus knew he would bring Lazarus back. Additionally, why would Jesus bereave in the face of his own looming death? When you think about it, very shortly he could eternally be with his dead friend if Lazarus remained deceased). Some suggest the lack of faith in the power of Christ over death among those present was the cause of his sorrow—much as he wept over Jerusalem for her lack of faith in Luke 19:41-42. (The problem with this is that faith in Jesus' ability to act even *post mortem* where Lazarus was concerned had been boldly expressed in Martha's statement, "But I know that even now God will give you whatever you ask" [v. 22]). The final reason offered for Jesus' tears, and the one that makes the most sense in the context, has to do with the empathy of Christ. He wept because he saw others weeping. As the identifying Son of Man, Jesus sympathized with the genuine hurting that these mourners felt. While Jesus' impending actions would soon turn their mourning into joy, in the moment he shared their pain.

89

The empathy of Christ still extends to those who are his friends today. The Hebrews writer reminds us that Jesus—now in his resurrected and ascended state—is "a high priest who is able to sympathize with our weaknesses" (Hebrews 4:15). Furthermore, he continues to empathize with us through the Spirit whom he left to live within us. In promising him, Jesus even spoke of the Holy Spirit as "the Comforter" (John 14:16,26; 15:26 and 16:7 in KJV), *paracletos* meaning "one who is called alongside to encourage and comfort."

No one is exempt from the pain of death, whether in dying oneself or in bereaving those who have passed. The comforting promises and presence of Christ are most helpful—even essential—in those moments. If you are a Christian you can confidently claim them.

The power of death is conquered by Jesus.

In his conversation with Martha Jesus revealed the paradigm-changing truth that he himself is "the resurrection and the life," further declaring, "He who believes in me will live even though he dies; and whoever lives and believes in me will never die" (vv. 25-26). By raising Lazarus from death after four days, Jesus would demonstrate the truth that he has proclaimed to Martha. Jesus personally holds power over death for all. In fact, Dwight Moody conjectured that "if our Lord had not called 'Lazarus' the place would have been filled with resurrected men!"[9] Perhaps this is so, but Jesus' calling of his name was just as well for the purpose of giving witness to his power for the individual in death. If Jesus could resurrect Lazarus—dead and buried for four days—then he can do the same for anyone.

In the gospels the raising of Lazarus is portrayed as the climactic miracle performed by Jesus during his ministry. While he had brought others back from death—namely Jairus' daughter and the widow of Nain's son—no miracle by Jesus was more dramatic or undeniable as the reviving of his dear friend at Bethany. It provided irrefutable proof of Jesus'

---

[9] Ronald Ward, *Proclaiming the New Testament, Vol. VII* (Grand Rapids, MI: Baker Book House, 1961), p. 75.

ultimate power over death. This miracle also proved to be the "last straw" with the Jewish religious leaders where Jesus was concerned. While not being able to deny the reality of this miracle, they made the final determination to kill him in response to it (John 11:45-57).

So, in a sense Lazarus' death points to Jesus' death, but Lazarus' resurrection also points to Jesus' resurrection by which he would, in an even more encompassing fashion, exercise his power over death; for, unlike Lazarus, Jesus would be raised never to die again, and with the power of extending this eternal resurrection to all who believe in him. The apostle Paul clearly enunciated this doctrine in the great resurrection chapter of the bible, 1 Corinthians 15, where he wrote,

> But Christ has indeed been raised from the dead, the firstfruits
> of those who have fallen asleep. For since death came through
> a man, the resurrection of the dead comes also through a man.
> For as in Adam all die, so in Christ all will be made alive. But
> each in his own turn: Christ, the firstfruits; then, when he
> comes, those who belong to him. (vv. 20-23)

The power of Christ over death was innate within him because he was God in the flesh. He was and is the very source of life and all things. The same voice that declared "Let there be light" in Genesis 1:3, resulting in light becoming an existing force, declared "Lazarus, come out!" resulting in a miraculous return to life from death. The same breath that breathed life into Adam penetrated the tomb where Lazarus' corpse lay, reuniting his soul and body. Jesus' deity was behind his assertion, "I am the resurrection and the life." May it be noted that even the "I am" statement here—as elsewhere evident in the "I am" statements of Jesus in John's gospel (cf.6:35; 8:12; 10:9,11; 14:6; 15:5)—pointed back to Jesus' identification with "Yahweh," the revealed name of God in the Old Testament. The power of death was conquered by Christ because he is the very Source of life.

Conclusion

I once read about a man who hosted a party in his home. Among his guests was a friend of his who was a surgeon. At the meal table, as the host began to carve the meat, he turned to the physician and asked, "How am I doing, doc? How do you like my technique? I'd make a pretty good surgeon, don't you think?"

When the host finished and the meat slices lay neatly on the serving platter, the surgeon responded to his previous boast: "Anybody can take them apart, Harry. Now let's see you put them back together again."[10]

There is good news for the sufferers of death—whether for those who personally face its prospects (which is eventually all of us) or those who are pained by the loss of a loved one (which we also all experience): Jesus has the power to put us back together again! The raising of Lazarus serves as convincing testimony to the truth that he is, indeed, "the resurrection and the life!"

Life Questions

1. When speaking to his disciples of Lazarus' passing, what metaphor does Jesus use to speak of death? _____

2. How is death for the Christian described in the following verses?
   –Psalm 116:15 _____
   –Luke 16:22 _____
   –Luke 23:43 _____
   –2 Corinthians 5:8 _____
   –Philippians 1:21 _____
   –Philippians 1:23 _____
   –Revelation 14:13 _____

---

[10] Adapted from Steve Shepherd, *The Importance of the Resurrection*, sermon at sermoncentral.com.

3. **Thought Question:** Why do you think Jesus wept (v. 35) at the tomb
   of Lazarus? _____

   _____

   _____

4. **Thought Question:** Of whom, specifically, do you think Jesus is
   speaking in verse 26 when he declares that "they will never die."

   _____

   _____

5. What is a (or are some) passage(s) of Scripture that you have found
   particularly helpful in times of loss/bereavement? _____

   _____

   _____

   _____

   _____

Good News for the Skeptic

—Thomas—

(John 20:19-29)

Introduction

A story at Bible.org relates the following account:

> On April 26, 1997, a student from Eagle Rock Junior High School in Idaho Falls, Idaho, won the first prize at the greater Idaho Falls Science Fair. He was attempting to show how conditioned we have become to alarmists practicing junk science and spreading fear of everything in our environment. The premise of his project was to urge people to sign a petition demanding strict control or total elimination of the chemical "dihydrogen monoxide;" and for plenty of good reasons, since
>
> 1. It can cause excessive sweating or vomiting.
> 2. It is a major component in acid rain.
> 3. It can cause severe burns in its gaseous state.
> 4. Accidental inhalation of it can kill you.
> 5. It decreases effectiveness of automobile brakes.
> 6. It has been found in tumors of terminal cancer patients.
>
> In his project the student asked 50 people if they supported a ban of the chemical. Of them, 43 said yes, six were undecided, and only one knew that this "dangerous" chemical was merely H_2O (water). The title of his prize-winning project was "How Gullible Are We?" The student felt the conclusion was obvious: we are very gullible.[1]

---

[1] Illustration from Bible.org/illustration/how-gullible-are-we

The Gem State is not the only place where people are gullible. I also recently read an account of a man in Radnor, Pennsylvania, who was interrogated as a possible suspect in a crime. In hopes of eliciting a confession from him the detectives placed a metal colander on the man's head and connected it with wires to a photocopy machine. (Yes, this one belongs in the category of "dumbest criminals.") The message "He's lying" was placed in the copier, and each time the cops thought the subject wasn't telling the truth an officer pressed the copy button and the machine spat out a sheet indicating the same. Believing the "lie detector" was real, the suspect confessed.[2]

We do live in a very gullible society—and the phenomenon transcends the borders of Idaho and Pennsylvania. From believing fake news reports to accepting the claims of junk science to the repeating of conspiracy theories, gullibility abounds. Many among us believe, among other far-fetched claims,

1. The moon landing was faked.
2. Elvis didn't really die on August 16, 1977.
3. Ancient aliens landed on earth and built the pyramids and other ancient structures.
4. Aliens planted life on earth. (Even one so "intelligent" as the militant atheist Richard Dawkins touts this claim.)
5. The earth is flat. (Yes, the Flat Earth Society is still around and has a membership of about 500 in the United States.)

While some people tend to believe any claim that is put in front of them, others are hesitant to believe any assertion that is made to them by others as a claim of truth; we call them "skeptics." Among those in the latter category was even one of Jesus' closest friends and disciples: Thomas. We usually refer to him as "doubting Thomas" because of his demonstrated reticence to believe when confronted with the claim of Christ's resurrection. In our study of him we will focus on the following three themes that surface in the account found in John 20:19-29: the

---

[2] Story from laughingnowamerica.com.

person who was the skeptic, the *patience of God* for the skeptic and the *promise of Jesus* for willing believers.

The Person Who Was a Skeptic

The gospels do not supply us with a lot of information about Thomas. While he is listed among the apostles in all of the lists in the synoptic gospels and Acts, the only details we have of him appear in the Gospel of John. These details are minute and sporadic. Here's what we do know of Thomas:

He was a twin. John twice notes that he was called "didymus" (in John 11:16 and 20:24) which means "twin." As to the identity of his twin we have no clue. Was it one of the other apostles? Was it another, unnamed disciple of Jesus? Was it someone who did not ultimately share the faith of his close sibling? Was Thomas' twin still living? Had he/she died in childhood? We simply do not know.

He was not always radically skeptical. You may recall that when Jesus expressed his plan to go back to the Jerusalem area to raise Lazarus---which, due to the threats of the Jewish religious leaders would likely mean death for Jesus---it was Thomas who alone spoke up, saying to the rest of the disciples, "Let us also go, that we may die with him" (John 11:16). His words here reveal a confidence that Jesus offered something greater than the fear of death for his followers. Of course, like most of us (and most of the other disciples) Thomas seems to have been stronger in his faith at certain times than he was at others.

He wasn't one who was willing to accept things blindly. When Jesus promised his disciples that he would be going to his Father's house to prepare a place for them and that he eventually would come back and take them to be with him, he concluded with the assumptive statement, "You know the way to the place where I am going" (John 14:1-4). Subsequently it was Thomas who immediately insisted to Jesus, "Lord, we don't know where you are going, so how can we know the way?" (v. 5)

Jesus assured Thomas with his answer in verse 6, "I am the way and the truth and the life." (i.e. "Just keep following me and you don't have to worry about the logistics regarding how you will get to where I am going.") This episode reveals Thomas as one who wasn't afraid to insist on further details and clarification of a claim—even one from the Lord---in order for him to accept it.

Once he was truly convinced of something, he was ready and willing to act on that belief. As previously noted, Thomas had once declared his willingness to die in going to Jerusalem with Jesus; and in our text, once he was confronted with the risen Lord—once he saw the scars from Jesus' nail-pierced hands and placed his hand in Jesus' side where the spear had recently pierced him—Thomas didn't hesitate with his declarative response: "My Lord, and My God!" These words reflected Thomas' personal worship of and submission to Jesus in that moment. This was a confession that would change the direction of Thomas' life from here on out because now he knew without a doubt that Jesus had defeated death!

The Patience of God for Skeptics

I am constantly amazed at the variety of people God called and used for his purposes in the record of the Scriptures. Even among the apostles there was quite a spectrum of personalities and positions: from Judas the betrayer to John the beloved; from Simon the Zealot (who sought military rebellion against Rome) to Matthew the tax-collector (who worked for Rome); from Peter, who often blindly declared his faith, to Thomas who famously doubted via his spirit of skepticism.

But Thomas wasn't the only skeptic God ever selected to do his bidding. He wasn't the only one who doubted when God asked for his or her trust. Consider Abraham who doubted God's promise that he would father a child in his agedness (Genesis 17:17-18). Sara, his wife, also doubted the same promise from God regarding herself (Genesis 18:12). Moses was more than skeptical about God's intended use of him to deliver Israel from Egyptian slavery (Exodus 3-4). The judge Gideon also doubted that God could use one such as him to "save Israel out of Midian's hand" (Judges 6:14-16,36-40). In the New Testament Martha, the sister of Lazarus, doubted that it was a good idea to open up Lazarus' tomb after he had been dead for four days, even though this was what Jesus commanded (John 11:38-40). Ananias of Damascus fearfully doubted God's ability to convert Saul to become his chosen vessel to take the gospel to the Gentiles (Acts 9:10-16).

Yet in all of these circumstances God proved his patience with the doubters. He was longsuffering toward these skeptics. Abraham and Sarah would, in God's time, have Isaac. God provided Moses with miracles to establish his authority and his brother to be his voice. He patiently responded to Gideon by granting him every sign of assurance for which he asked. He had the stone of Lazarus' tomb rolled back anyway—without arguing with Martha—and she reaped the benefit of having her beloved dead brother returned to her. For Ananias the Lord patiently assured that this was indeed his purpose regarding Saul. He could be confident in being God's human instrument involved in Saul's conversion.

This overview of biblical skeptics could not be complete without considering the account of the man in Mark 9 whose son was possessed by an evil spirit. The disciples had tried, but even though they had been successful in other exorcisms, they could not cast out this demon. The subsequent conversation of the boy's father with Jesus follows:

> "...if you can do anything, take pity on us and help us."
>
> "'If you can?'" said Jesus. "Everything is possible for him who believes."
>
> Immediately the boy's father exclaimed, "I do believe; help me overcome my unbelief!" (Mark 9:22b-24)

Jesus did help him in overcoming his unbelief by healing his son; thus, Jesus met this man at the point of his existing faith. In this we witness Jesus, as God in the flesh, demonstrating patience and mercy toward this man in his skepticism. Jesus did the same for Thomas in our text. He didn't confront Thomas about his disbelief or question him as to his absence among the apostles on the former occasion that he had appeared to them. He didn't even chastise him for not believing the testimony of the other apostles. He didn't call him "thick-headed" or even "doubting

Thomas." He met him where he was and patiently showed him the proofs for which he asked, leaving Thomas with no doubt about Jesus' victory over death.

The Promise of Jesus to Willing Believers

It is often stated that "seeing is believing." In truth, that maxim isn't always correct. Magicians can make things appear as reality (and have been doing so for centuries) that are not reality at all. Modern computer technology makes it possible for photographs to be digitally doctored to present images that are not genuine. Believing what our eyes see isn't always possible; however, admittedly, personally witnessing an event through physical observance can certainly aid us in determining whether something is or is not real. Thomas saw with his eyes the proof of the Lord's resurrection; yet even Jesus acknowledged that there was still some level of faith involved in Thomas' acceptance of it as fact. He stated to Thomas, "Because you have seen me, you have believed." Even with the empirical observation Thomas experienced, some leap of faith was still required of him. Granted, it was a much shorter leap than it would have been if he had not seen the risen Lord, observed the nail scars in his hands and put his hand into the very place that the centurion's spear had plunged. Indeed, it seems to me it would have been a much longer leap of faith for Thomas to remain in his doubt once he had witnessed these things.

After commending Thomas for his faith-based-on-sight, Jesus then honored, in beatific language, those who would not enjoy the privilege of empirically witnessing him in his risen state, yet who would still believe. There were many among Jesus' earliest followers who did get to witness his resurrected body. These included Mary Magdalene, all of the apostles, the Lord's brother James, and many other disciples. Paul even informs us that, on one occasion, "he appeared to more than 500 of the brothers at the same time" (1 Corinthians 15:6). Yet, the majority of those who would claim faith in Christ's resurrection—even those living in the first century—did not personally observe the risen Lord. They, like all in subsequent generations of Christians (including ours), would believe based upon the testimony of those who did get to see him. Jesus pronounced all such believers as "blessed" because they "have not seen and yet have believed." (v. 29)

Jesus' blessing upon those who would believe in his resurrection, not by first-hand experience but via the testimony of those who claimed that experience, is due to the greater leap of faith that they (we) would have to take. Yet, it must be noted that the testimony of those who claimed witness to Jesus' resurrection was accompanied by actions that intensely underscored their claims. Many of them (including all but John among the apostles) would experience martyrs' deaths for the claim that Jesus had risen from the dead. Given the overall evidence of their testimony, one might even contend that, while it takes a greater leap of faith for non-witnesses to believe the claim of the resurrection, in the end it may very well require—as was noted of Thomas once he witnessed the proofs that he did—a greater leap of faith for one to walk away from the evidence of Jesus' resurrection without believing in it. Jesus' promise of blessing remains for those who, on this basis, do believe.

Conclusion

I am glad that the gospel account includes the record of a skeptic among the disciples. Thomas' reticence to believe reveals to us that the resurrection of Christ was not a matter of collective wishful thinking; even among these close followers of Jesus it was a matter that required proof. That proof was provided and Thomas became one of the most credible advocates of the resurrection. Among the apostles he took the gospel geographically farther than any other—all the way to India.

Often those, like Thomas, who begin with the despair of doubt, become the strongest defenders of the claims of the gospel once they believe. The most convincing voices among Christian apologists have been and remain today those who struggled through the journey of doubt and skepticism. Their names are familiar: Lew Wallace (who out of his experience wrote the classic book *Ben Hur: A Tale of the Christ*), the archeologist Sir William Ramsey, C.S. Lewis, Josh McDowell, Charles

Colson, Gary Habermas, Lee Strobel and J. Warner Wallace, among others.

It is possible, given the presentation of convincing evidence, for a skeptic to change his mind. For over 20 years I had suffered from debilitating pain caused by *plantar fasciitis* in my left heel. I had tried everything but surgery (which was not recommended by my doctor) to alleviate this pain that often made it difficult for me to walk. Years of exercise and therapy sessions did not seem to help. Painful steroid shots in the foot provided only temporary relief as did anti-inflammatory drugs. The wearing of expensive and uncomfortable therapeutic boots at night to stretch the tendon had little to no positive effect. While discussing my frustration about this one day with my general practitioner he said, "Well, you know, Tim, they have been having some helpful results with acupuncture for *plantar fasciitis*;" and after warning me that my insurance would probably not pay for it, he asked, "Would you consider trying it?"

Not being a connoisseur of alternative medicine, I wore my doubtful response with folded arms: "Oh, why not give it a try—nothing else has worked."

I had my first session with the acupuncturist a week later. After I pointed out the specific region of my pain in my left heel, she began placing needles—eight to ten of them—into my right palm. As she proceeded also to stick needles into the exterior of my left ear (and yes, it hurt) she explained to me the history of acupuncture and how through the centuries practitioners had mapped out trigger spots for the body's nerve system which, when manipulated, would affect other areas of the body.

After about 35 uncomfortable minutes the acupuncturist removed the needles one at a time. When she was finished, she asked me to walk across the room to her, informing her how my heel felt. Commencing my walk, I stated with honesty, "Well, I'm still feeling a lot of pain."

She nodded.

However, about halfway across the fifteen-foot room I volunteered my new sensation: "But...I'm experiencing what feels like a warm waterfall over my left heel."

101

"That's the blood flowing there in a way that it hasn't for a while—it's also exactly what I hoped you would tell me," she said.

From that moment the pain in my left heel began to ebb. In that entire week it never got above about a two or three on the pain scale. The needle process was repeated when I saw her on the following Friday (only now with an additional probing of my left pinkie finger). After that session, the pain was essentially gone; and after the third and final session a week later it was entirely gone. It has now been more than four years since those treatments, and I have not even once experienced the pain that had been so familiar to me for over 20 years. I was admittedly a doubter and a skeptic when it came to acupuncture; now I am convinced of its claims. My mind was changed by my experience.

Thomas' mind was changed by his experience, too; he had seen the risen Lord. The minds of many skeptics of the gospel who haven't experienced the privilege of first-hand observation have also been changed because they took the time and care to look into the evidence for Christ's claims.

If you are such a skeptic, I challenge you to look into these same claims. I challenge you to study the biographies and writings of the aforementioned doubters who became believers and apologists. I challenge you to give the evidence regarding Christ and his resurrection the consideration it deserves for your life—and for your eternity.

Life Questions

1. What two things did Thomas immediately do when he was convinced of the reality of Jesus' resurrection? _____
   _____
   _____
   _____

2. Who are some people in the bible, other than Thomas, who exhibited doubt with God? _____

_____

_____

_____

3. Can you think of someone you personally know who may be considered a skeptic? _____ If yes, how have they demonstrated their skepticism to you? _____

_____

_____

4. Have you ever received good news that you were skeptical to believe at first? _____ Why were you hesitant to believe it? _____

_____

_____

Did you come to believe it eventually? _____ If so, what caused you to change your mind? _____

_____

_____

5. What are some powerful proofs of the gospel that might be presented to the skeptics of our time? _____

_____

_____

Good News for the Stumbler

—Simon Peter—

(John 21:15-23)

Introduction

One of my favorite stories that depicts both the controlling power of sin in our lives and the freedom that comes from experiencing forgiveness is one that was originally shared by Richard C. Hoefler in his book *Will Daylight Come? Background on the Miracles* (C.S.S. Publishing Co., 1979):

A little boy who was visiting his grandparents was given his first slingshot. He practiced in the woods, but he could never hit his target. As he came into his grandma's back yard, he spied her pet duck. On an impulse he took aim and let it fly. The stone hit its target and the duck fell dead. The boy panicked. Desperately he hid the dead duck in the wood pile, only to look up and see his sister watching. Sally had seen it all, but she said nothing.

After lunch that day, Grandma said, "Sally, let's wash the dishes." But Sally said, "Johnny told me he wanted to help in the kitchen today. Didn't you Johnny?" And she whispered to him, "Remember the duck!" So Johnny did the dishes.

Later Grandpa asked if the children wanted to go fishing. Grandma said, "I'm sorry, but I need Sally to help make supper." Sally smiled and said, "That's all taken care of. Johnny wants to do it." Again she whispered, "Remember the duck." Johnny stayed while Sally went fishing.

After several days of Johnny doing both his chores and Sally's, finally he couldn't stand it. He confessed to Grandma that he'd killed the duck. "I know, Johnny," she said, giving him a hug. "I was standing at the window and saw the whole thing. Because I love you, I forgave you. I wondered how long you would let Sally make a slave of you."[1]

Like the boy in the story, Simon Peter was poised to become a slave to his failure in denying Christ three times; but John 21 relates to us the intriguing account of Jesus' conversation with Peter through which he restored him in his discipleship and his personal relationship with him. He also re-commissioned him regarding his calling as an apostle by commanding him to "feed /take care of my lambs/sheep" as well as in informing him as to what his future plans were for Peter (vv. 18-19). This is the first and only one-on-one dialogue recorded of Jesus with Peter after he committed his denials of the Lord in the courtyard of the high priest after Jesus' arrest. (While it should be noted that Jesus had personally appeared to Peter on the day of his resurrection as revealed in Luke 24:34, the gospels provide no record of any conversation between Peter and Jesus at that point.)

Peter needed restoration. He had greatly fallen from his height as a disciple who was adamantly vocal in his commitment to Jesus. He was guilty of sin in denying his relationship with Jesus. He was in danger of Jesus now denying him before his heavenly Father per the Lord's previous warning of Matthew 10:33: "But whoever disowns me before men, I will disown him before my Father in heaven." Peter needed the Lord's forgiveness for his stumbling into sin through the denials. It was only through forgiveness that Peter could be restored in his discipleship and apostleship. While Jesus' forgiveness of Peter is not explicitly stated in this passage, it is clearly implied within their conversation.

The Response Jesus Desired from Peter

Jesus began this conversation with Peter by asking Peter to reaffirm his love for him. He submitted to him essentially the same question three times: "Simon...do you love me?" I am confident that Jesus was intentional in presenting three inquiries regarding Peter's love for him to

---

[1] Illustration as told at Bible.org.

harken back to the three denials that Peter had committed. (These are recorded in John 18:15-17, 25-27.) When you think about it, there are so many other things Jesus could have said to him at this time: "Well, Peter, I told you you'd do it." "Simon, you really hurt me when you denied me!" "Peter, are you sorry for what you did?"—I suppose he could have asked *that* three times; instead he asked about his love for him three times.

Why was Jesus' expressed concern in this moment all about Peter's love for him? This is because Jesus is always concerned about his followers' love for him. Love is to be the primary motive by which anyone who follows Jesus should be driven to do so. After all, the gospel itself is a love story; it is a love story that begins with God's love toward us in sending his Son into our realm to redeem us from sin. Jesus most familiarly portrayed it as such to Nicodemus when he spoke of his incarnation by stating that "God so loved the world that he gave his one and only Son..." (John 3:16a). The apostle John would later summarize our ideal response to Christ through the gospel succinctly with these words: "We love because he first loved us." (1 John 4:19)

There are other motivations than love out of which we can come to Christ. For instance, we can come to him out of fear. It is true that we should fear God; Jesus stressed this in Matthew 10:28 with his command to his disciples "...be afraid of the One who can destroy both soul and body in hell." However, the bible teaches that love should trump even fear in our relationship with God. This is indicated in John's statement in 1 John 4:18: "There is no fear in love. But perfect love drives out fear, because fear has to do with punishment. The one who fears is not made perfect in love."

We can also come to God out of religious tradition. Yet, while it is good to be raised in a family in which faith in God and commitment to Christ is taught—even passed down to some degree—such faith can only take us so far in Christ. Somewhere along the way each individual believer must develop his or her own appreciation of God's love for him or her and personally respond to it in kind. This is what Christ desires of us.

One can even come to God motivated by pride. The pursuit of righteousness can be motivated by the perception of self-righteousness.

106

Yet, given Jesus' strong indictments of the religious leaders of his day for being motivated by pride, it should be clear to us that this is never a good motivation for the pursuit of godliness. Love is to be the primary motivation that should drive us toward God, and love promotes humility, thus diminishing our tendencies toward pride.

One way Jesus taught that love was to be our primary reason for responding to him was in his answer to the question raised to him by the expert in the law in Matthew 22:35-40:

> One of them, an expert in the law, tested him with this question: "Teacher, which is the greatest commandment in the Law?"
>
> Jesus replied, "'Love the Lord your God with all your heart and with all your soul and with all your mind.' This is the first and greatest commandment. And the second is like it, 'Love your neighbor as yourself.' All the Law and the prophets hang on these two commandments."

In John 21, Peter was reminded by Jesus of his need to follow him and serve him out of love more than any other motivation. He certainly had reason to fear the Lord's judgment at this time, but Jesus elevated love over that fear. He certainly had a faith tradition, but he was not to rely on that. He had some prideful motivations behind some of his previous boasting regarding his commitment to Christ (Matthew 26:33), but his pride could now be thrown to the wayside.

Additionally, I sense that Jesus expressed his desire for Peter's love as a way of reminding Peter that, despite his recent failures, Jesus still loved *him*. This is surely what Peter needed to know at this point, and this is what we often need to be reminded of when we have failed in our commitment to Christ. Christ's love for us is so strong, so steadfast and so forgiving that nothing can separate us from it (Romans 8:37-39)—not even our failures.

Within Jesus' inquiry regarding Peter's love for him, we must not miss the comparative reference as to whether Simon loved him "more than these?" The "these" to which Jesus referred could be the *objects* of Peter's affection: namely the fishing gear and livelihood that Simon knew so well, or even these other disciples who were his partners and friends (a brother in the case of Andrew). Another, more probable, interpretation makes "these" co-*subjects* in love for Christ—namely the other disciples by comparison. Thus, the intent of Jesus was to ask, "Do you love me more than these other disciples love me?" In the light of Peter's prior verbal commitment that "Even if all fall away...I never will" (Matthew 26:33), this is the probable meaning of "more than these."

Finally, it should be noted that in his response Peter made a strong affirmation of his love for the Lord. Much has been made of the language choice Peter used in his answers to Jesus' questions. It is often argued that there was an implicit reticence by Peter here because of his consistent use of *phileo* in his responses, while Jesus, in the first two inquiries, has used *agapao*. The assumption is that *phileo* describes a lower level of love than *agapao*. Yet, the former word implies a love of "warmth and closeness and affection", while the latter implies more of an "at large" love[2]—the kind that Jesus' disciples can, and must, have for all mankind. For example, in the preface to the parable of the good Samaritan Jesus used *agapao* in the command for his followers to "Love your neighbor as yourself" in Luke 10:27. Thus, this is the kind of love one can harbor toward even a strange "neighbor" who has been robbed, beaten and left for dead. (See Luke 10:25-37.) I contend that Simon Peter used the *stronger* word. His was not just an "at large" love for his Lord; it was the love of a personal friendship—a "brotherly love" as inferred from *phileo*. And, when you think about it, isn't it like Simon—impetuous as he was— to verbally stress this more intense level of relationship with Jesus? It was as though he was begging for Jesus to see him once again, not just as one who followed him and loved him in general as a disciple, but in terms of the personal friendship they enjoyed. In the end Jesus met Peter at the level of *phileo* as he too employed this word in his final inquiry.

---

[2] Paul Butler, *The Gospel of John, Vol. 1*, p. 456.

The Reception Jesus Demonstrated to Peter

Each time Jesus responded to Peter's affirmation of his love he did so with a command: "Feed my lambs" (v. 15); "Take care of my sheep" (v. 16); and "Feed my sheep" (v. 17). Through these directives Jesus seems to be reminding Peter that to love him is to serve him. With each of the claims of love that Peter made Jesus commanded him to do something—namely to serve him in the role of shepherding his followers. This is a principle that is applicable to all of Jesus' followers; one's professed love for Christ is attested to by submission to his will for one's life. Jesus expressed this truth concisely in John 14:15: "If you love me, you will obey what I command." It is one thing to say we love Jesus, but such a claim for love must be borne out in actions.

William Henry Harrison was the ninth president of the United States. When he was inaugurated in 1840, he had prepared a very lengthy (9,000 word) inaugural address. The day of his inauguration arrived with inclement weather—it was dismal, cold and wet. Despite this fact, Harrison stubbornly insisted on delivering the entirety of his speech, which lasted almost two hours. In this effort, the new president caught pneumonia and within a month he was dead. Resultantly, William Henry Harrison holds two presidential records: one for the longest speech and another for the shortest term served of any president. His words were many; his actions ended up being very few. Hence, his many words meant very little.[3]

It is easy to speak words expressing love for and commitment to Jesus; but to make them ring true they must be accompanied by actions of obedience and service to him. Peter needed to be reminded of this and often we do, too.

Additionally, Jesus was reminding Peter of the specific job that he had for him to do. Peter was still the leader among his disciples and his apostles. He would still be utilizing the "keys of the kingdom" that Jesus had personally promised him (Matthew 16:19). In short, despite his failure

---

[3] Benjamin Lampkin, "7 Presidential Facts About William Henry Harrison," mentalfloss.com, October 12, 2015.

in his denials, Jesus wasn't done with Peter yet. In a sense Peter should have already known this. You may recall that the angel at the empty tomb had instructed Mary Magdalene and the other women to "...go, tell his disciples and Peter, 'He is going ahead of you into Galilee'" (Mark 16:7). From the moment of his resurrection Jesus wanted Peter—especially Peter—to know about it and be aware of his future plans.

Jesus' planned use of Peter tells us that he had forgiven this denier of his crimes. When did Jesus forgive Peter? Perhaps he did so before he even committed the denials; after all, the Lord had made it clear that he knew Peter was going to commit them. Perhaps he forgave him on the heels of the final denial, when, as revealed in Luke 22:61-62,

> The Lord turned and looked straight at Peter, then Peter re-
> membered the word the Lord had spoken to him: "Before
> the rooster crows today, you will disown me three times."
> And he went out and wept bitterly.

Did Jesus recognize in Peter's tears the "godly sorrow that brings repentance" (2 Corinthians 7:10) thus forgiving him in that moment? Or was it in the encounter in our text that Christ's pardon—though not stated but certainly implied—was extended to Peter? While we cannot know when the moment of his forgiveness took place, we can be certain of the reality of it for Peter; for only in the remitting of his sin could he, once again, be the appropriate vessel of service that the Lord intended him to be.

I prefer that Jesus' pardoning of Peter was immediate to his denials—as though Jesus couldn't wait to forgive Peter and it was his desire to do so. It is always his desire to forgive us when we fail him—a truth that we must never forget as Christians. Sadly, I sense that with many of Jesus' followers, self-forgiveness for failures often takes longer than the ready remission of our sins through Christ. It seems we tend to give up on ourselves much more quickly than God gives up on us. Perhaps Peter was feeling such sentiments of spiritual inadequacy at this point. Maybe this is why Jesus seemingly goes out of his way to have this one-on-one

110

conversation with Peter in this setting—to make him aware of the reality of his forgiveness and the Lord's future usefulness of him.

The Responsibility Jesus Demanded of Peter

Along with the good news of forgiveness and reinstatement to his calling that Peter received from Jesus, there was also some not-so-good-news for him. In fact, it more precisely may be dubbed "bad news." It is found in verse 18 where Jesus, rather cryptically, revealed to Peter that he will eventually die a martyr's death for Christ's cause. These are Jesus' words to him:

> I tell you the truth, when you were younger you dressed your-
> self and went where you wanted; but when you are old you will
> stretch out your hands, and someone else will dress you and
> lead you where you do not want to go.

How much Peter grasped Jesus' meaning when he stated this prophecy, we cannot be sure. Did he realize Jesus might be describing Peter's own death by crucifixion—which was the means by which tradition tells us he was martyred by the Romans—when he spoke of him forcibly stretching out his hands? Jesus did say this was an experience he understandably would not want to go through, and Peter did seem to discern enough regarding Jesus' allusion to his future death that he clearly didn't want to know any more details about this prophecy. Instead, he quickly and conveniently changed the subject, putting the focus on his fellow-apostle, John.

The competitive nature of Peter and John's relationship within the apostolic band is evident within the gospels. There was definitely a spirit of rivalry between them. While Peter had been promised personally by Jesus that he would possess the "keys of the kingdom," James and John sought to vie for the positions of sitting on Jesus' right and left in his kingdom with their request (via their mother) in Matthew 20:20-21. An indication of this personal competitiveness is also inferred from John 20:3-4 where the writer, John, bragged about he and Peter both arriving at the tomb of Jesus after Mary Magdalene reported it to be empty: "So Peter and the other disciple [John] started for the tomb. Both were running, but the other disciple outran Peter and reached the tomb first." Now why mention that detail if there wasn't some rivalry going on? John was boasting that he was faster than Peter in a notation of physical one-upmanship. But the spirit of rivalry went both ways; thus, we witness Peter immediately turning the spotlight to John with Jesus by asking (in light of his own future bad news), "[but] Lord, what about *him*?" (v. 21--- emphasis mine)

Jesus' answer to Peter, recorded in verse 22, was two-fold: first, he made it clear that what he would require of John's life in service to him was, frankly, none of Peter's business: "If I want him to remain alive until I return, what is that to you?" Second, Peter was to focus on the responsibilities Jesus intended for *him*: "You must follow me." Jesus had already commanded this of Peter at the end of verse 19, but now he reiterated it with the emphatic (in the Greek) "*you* follow me." The message was clear: Peter was only to be responsible for what Jesus was asking him to do; he wasn't to be concerned with what would be required of John. The same is true regarding our calling to personal service for our Lord. We are only responsible for ourselves. No one else is responsible to accomplish what Christ is calling you or me to do; and you or I are not responsible for what Christ is calling someone else to do. We cannot fulfill their obligations to the Lord; neither can they fulfill ours.

As John editorially notes, Jesus' answer to Peter about John resulted in an item of misinformation that was spread among the early Christians as indicated in verse 23:

> Because of this, the rumor spread among the brothers that this
> disciple would not die. But Jesus did not say that he would
> not die; he only said, "If I want him to remain alive until I return,
> what is that to you?"

One can only imagine that John, writing this gospel perhaps well into his 80s, knew full well that he was not meant to hang around in his flesh for an indeterminate amount of time. He was quite concerned about

112

quashing this misunderstanding about what Jesus had said regarding him. In fact, the consensus of scholarship agrees that chapter 21 of John's gospel—replete with its positive portrayal of the writer's rival—was entirely added for the purpose of making this clarification. Verses 30-31 of chapter 20 had offered, after all, a natural conclusion to this volume with its stated purpose:

> Jesus did many other miraculous signs in the presence of his disciples, which are not recorded in this book. But these are written that you may believe that Jesus is the Christ, the Son of God, and that by believing you may have life in his name.

Conclusion

In his book *More Sower's Seeds: Second Planting*, author Brian Cavanaugh relates the story about a man who risked his life by swimming through the treacherous riptide to save a youngster who was being swept out to sea. When they were back on the shore, after the child recovered from the harrowing experience, he said to the man, "Thank you for saving my life."

The man looked into the boy's eyes and said, "That's okay, kid. Just make sure your life was worth saving."[4]

The guilt and condemnation of the denials were wholly behind Peter now, and in forgiving Peter Jesus challenged him to a lifetime response to that forgiveness. We know from the later New Testament record that Peter was faithful in that response. He used the keys of the kingdom when, in Acts 2:14-40, he preached the first gospel sermon on the day of Pentecost resulting in 3,000 persons experiencing salvation in Christ for the first time. He used them again when he, instructed through a personal revelation from the Lord in Acts 10, was led to the house of Cornelius, who became the first Gentile to experience salvation in Christ. He became the recognized leader of the apostles (see Acts 15:7ff and Galatians 1:18; 2:7-9) and wrote two powerful letters to the churches

---

[4] Brian Cavanaugh, *More Sower's Seeds: Second Planting* (Mahwah, NJ: Paulist Press, 1992), pp. 767-77.

throughout Asia Minor encouraging them to godly living in the context of a world increasingly hostile to their faith in Christ. We know these as 1 Peter and 2 Peter. Ultimately, he did suffer the martyr's death which Jesus had prophesied when, about 64 AD, he was crucified in Rome. Herbert Lockyer notes of Peter's crucifixion:

> Meantime, it can be said that as his crucifiers came to end his honored career, he pleaded with them to hang him upside down because he deemed himself unworthy to die in the same position as his Lord had done.[5]

Life Questions

1. What are some Scripture verses that indicate that the primary motivation God desires for us to have in service to him is love? ____
   _____
   _____

2. What scriptural evidence points to Peter's repentance for his actions in denying Jesus? _____
   _____
   _____

3. Since we still have the same call from Jesus today to "follow me," but we cannot physically follow Jesus (as did the early disciples), what are some ways in which we can "follow" Jesus in our own time?
   _____
   _____
   _____
   _____

---

[5] Herbert Lockyer, *All the Apostles of the Bible* (Grand Rapids: MI: Zondervan, 1972), p. 149.

4. For what reason do biblical scholars believe that chapter 21 was an addition to the original Gospel of John? _____

_____

_____

5. What do you consider to be a specific task that Jesus has for you (and you only) to do?_____

_____

_____

Conclusion to this Study

Peter's encounter with Jesus in John 21 was every bit as life-changing as the first encounter he had had with Jesus earlier by Galilee when he heard the first call of Christ to "Come, follow me...and I will make you fishers of men." (Matthew 4:19). Indeed, all of the one-on-one encounters with Jesus we have focused on from John's gospel were intensely life-changing. The sincere Nathaniel would wholly surrender his life to Christ's cause. The seeker Nicodemus would find in Christ the fulfillment of all the law and prophets to which he had dedicated decades of study. The social outcast at Jacob's Well at Sychar would know acceptance and have access to "living water." The official who demonstrated submissive faith in Christ would see his son grow to manhood. The self-absorbed lame man would experience new physical freedom as well as a reason to stop sinning (and being so self-absorbed). The adulterous woman would find ultimate forgiveness with a powerful reason to leave her life of sin. The man who had known only sightlessness in a moment would gain vision---both physically and spiritually---for the first time and for the rest of his life. Lazarus and his sisters would experience the power of resurrection that is available in Christ. Thomas, the skeptic, would be left with no remaining reason to doubt and, as an apostle, would take the gospel geographically farther than any of the others (India). Finally, Peter would fulfill Christ's intended and lifelong purpose for him, including the martyrdom Jesus predicted.

While we cannot experience physical encounters with Christ today, we can still meet him one-on-one, as it were, through the gospel narratives in which he is revealed to us. I am convinced that when we, through these records, genuinely allow ourselves to experience Jesus of Nazareth—his claims, his forgiveness, his truth, his power—we too will be changed, and in the most dramatic and enduring of ways.

In Memoriam

1988-2018

This book is published in memory of Kelly Carlson Roberts who tragically left us too soon. Kelly was the daughter of the author. She leaves behind her family, her church family, and a host of friends. Most importantly, Kelly knew what it meant to have the good news of Jesus making its intended difference in her life.

www.ingramcontent.com/pod-product-compliance
Lightning Source LLC
Chambersburg PA
CBHW051812040426
42446CB00007B/639